The Deepfake Dilemma

Deepfakes are no longer a future threat, they are an operational reality.

The Deepfake Dilemma: Technology, Truth, and Forensic Integrity is a vital resource for professionals navigating the complex intersection of synthetic media, digital evidence, and investigative integrity. As deepfake technologies become increasingly sophisticated, accessible, and difficult to detect, their implications for criminal justice, legal accountability, and public trust are profound.

Unlike general-interest books that focus on the cultural novelty or sensational impact of deepfakes, *The Deepfake Dilemma* takes a forensic-centred, practitioner-focused approach. Written specifically for law enforcement officers, digital forensic analysts, legal professionals, and cybersecurity practitioners, this book delivers a structured, evidence-driven examination of how deepfakes are created, how they are detected, and how they are being weaponised in real-world criminal and investigative contexts.

With deepfake-enabled crimes (ranging from identity fraud and extortion to disinformation and evidential manipulation) reported to have increased dramatically since 2019, the need for practical investigative frameworks has never been more urgent. This book meets that need head-on through detailed case studies, forensic workflows, and applied methodologies grounded in professional practice.

Readers will learn how to:

- Detect and analyse synthetic media using both algorithmic and digital forensic techniques.
- Assess the credibility, provenance, and admissibility of digital media evidence.
- Apply investigative strategies to mitigate deepfake risks in criminal, legal, and organisational settings.

- Navigate the legal and ethical challenges posed by synthetic media, including evidentiary uncertainty and privacy concerns.

By bridging the gap between technical complexity and real-world application, *The Deepfake Dilemma* equips professionals with the tools and critical insight needed to safeguard evidential integrity in an era where seeing is no longer believing. Whether you are a digital investigator, legal practitioner, cybersecurity professional, or policymaker, this book is an indispensable guide to confronting the deepfake threat and defending truth in the age of synthetic media.

The Deepfake Dilemma
Technology, Truth, and Forensic Integrity

Dr Áine MacDermott

CRC Press
Taylor & Francis Group
Boca Raton London New York

CRC Press is an imprint of the
Taylor & Francis Group, an **informa** business

Designed cover image: Shutterstock ID: 1456783511

First edition published 2027
by CRC Press
2385 NW Executive Center Drive, Suite 320, Boca Raton FL 33431

and by CRC Press
4 Park Square, Milton Park, Abingdon, Oxon, OX14 4RN

CRC Press is an imprint of Taylor & Francis Group, LLC

ISBN: 9781041200499 (hbk)
ISBN: 9781041200505 (pbk)
ISBN: 9781003714811 (ebk)

DOI: 10.1201/9781003714811

Typeset in Caslon
by Newgen Publishing UK

Contents

About the Author

Dr Áine MacDermott is a Senior Lecturer in the School of Computer Science and Mathematics, at Liverpool John Moores University, specialising in digital forensics and cyber security. With over 14 years of research experience, Dr MacDermott has conducted impactful research-informed teaching involving forensic evidence handling and methodologies, IoT and smart devices, cyber security of IoT, and currently the analysis of fabricated media. Dr MacDermott holds a PhD in Network Security and BSc (Hons) in Computer Forensics and is passionate about educating the next generation of forensics professionals on the challenges and opportunities presented by emerging technologies like deepfakes. With over 50 academic publications to date, Dr MacDermott continues to contribute significantly to the fields of cyber security and digital forensics.

Dr MacDermott is a recognised expert in the intersection of cyber security and digital forensics of IoT devices and has spoken at numerous industry conferences and workshops. Dr MacDermott has been an Adjunct Professor at Ontario Tech University since 2020. In addition to her academic roles, she actively engages in public outreach and education, organising workshops such as a “Deepfake Forensics” event at LJMU in 2023, and Deepfake Forensics 2.0 in May 2026, which brought together professionals from academia and law enforcement to address challenges posed by AI-generated media.

She collaborates with external partners, including the Merseyside Police, Zayed University (Dubai), and Ontario Tech University (Canada). Her commitment to bridging academia and industry is further demonstrated by her contributions to national policy discussions; notably, she provided written expert testimony to the UK Parliament's Science, Innovation and Technology Select Committee on the impact of social media algorithms in spreading disinformation.

Preface

Modern society is entering an era where the line between reality and fabrication is increasingly difficult to discern. The authenticity of visual and audio evidence can no longer be assumed. Images, videos, and voices – once regarded as reliable records of truth – can now be fabricated with extraordinary precision. Deepfakes and other forms of synthetic media have moved beyond experimental curiosities; they have become powerful tools capable of influencing elections, damaging reputations, committing fraud, and undermining the very foundations of trust in public life.

This book examines the rapidly evolving field of deepfake forensics and the profound societal challenges it presents. At its heart lies a critical question: *how can we determine what is real in a world where reality itself can be convincingly forged?*

For law enforcement, deepfakes introduce new categories of crime and obstacles to investigation. Digital evidence can no longer be accepted at face value; every image, video, or audio clip may require additional expert scrutiny. Investigators must balance speed with rigor, adopting forensic techniques that can keep pace with increasingly sophisticated generative models.

For the courts, the stakes are even higher. Legal systems depend on reliable evidence, clear standards of admissibility, and the ability to explain complex technical findings to judges and juries. When authenticity itself is contested, long-standing assumptions about proof, credibility, and burden of evidence are strained. The question is no longer simply *what does the evidence show?* but *can the evidence be trusted at all?*

Beyond crime and justice, the implications for society are profound. Deepfakes erode public trust, amplify misinformation, and blur the line between satire, deception, and harm. They force us to confront uncomfortable truths about perception, cognitive bias, and our reliance on digital media as a shared record of events.

This book does not seek to provoke alarm, nor does it claim that technology alone can resolve the problems it creates. Instead, it aims to illuminate the technical foundations of deepfake generation and detection, the limitations of current forensic methods, and the legal, ethical, and institutional responses required to address them. It is written for practitioners and policymakers, researchers and students, journalists and informed citizens – anyone concerned with preserving truth, justice, and trust in the age of synthetic media.

The challenge of deepfakes is not merely a technical arms race between generation and detection. It is a societal test of resilience: our ability to adapt laws, institutions, and norms to a world where reality itself can be engineered. The pages that follow invite readers to understand this challenge and to engage thoughtfully with the responsibility it places on all of us.

Acknowledgements

I am deeply grateful to my family for their support and encouragement throughout this journey. I owe special thanks to my husband, Chris, for his meticulous proofreading and thoughtful advice, which greatly enhanced the clarity and quality of this work.

My heartfelt appreciation also goes to Salem for being a constant source of strength. To my amazing friends:thank you for patiently listening to countless stories about this book and cheering me on along the way. And to Dominique and Rachel for the many deepfakes we made testing out tools!

Finally, I am sincerely thankful to all who engaged with my research, shared their insights, and provided constructive feedback. Your contributions have been invaluable in shaping and refining this work.

AI Statement

- *Figure 2.2* This figure uses two real images (with permission from the individuals pictured). The faces were swapped using Remaker AI v2 Attribution: https://remaker.ai/face-swap-free/.
- *Figure 2.3* Elements of this figure were generated using ChatGPT-5 (generator image, database, fake/real sample) and then edited further using Microsoft Word shapes. AI Tool Attribution: I asked ChatGPT to create a similar image to *generative adversarial networks (GANs) diagram* (https://medium.com/@priyanshuprasad1718/artificial-faces-the-encoder-decoder-and-gan-guide-to-deepfakes-75a1eed0e265) but to have blurry female in the sample boxes. Then additional editing was completed in MS Word.
- *Figure 2.4* Created using Microsoft Copilot (GPT-5). A real photo of the author was uploaded, and Copilot generated an AI version and AI variants (frown, smile, closed eyes). AI Tool Attribution: Image created and facial expressions manipulated using M365 Copilot (GPT-5).
- *Figure 2.5* Created using Microsoft Copilot (GPT-5) by prompting it to generate an image stylistically similar to that

shown on the VALL-E project page (www.microsoft.com/en-us/research/project/vall-e-x/vall-e/).

- *Figure 5.1* uses aspects of my face swap in (Figure 2.4) and includes face morphing/attribute manipulation based on my own images.
- *Figure 7.5* Created using Chat GPT-5 following a prompt to: generate an image of a black cat drinking coffee. AI Tool Attribution: Image generated using M365 Copilot (GPT-5).
- *Figure 7.7* Edited using Microsoft Paint (version 11.2512.191.0).

Glossary

ACPO Guidelines (UK) ACPO Guidelines outline how digital evidence should be accessed, preserved, and examined to remain admissible, emphasising necessity, accountability, and integrity.

Admissibility A court's determination that evidence may be considered at trial, based on relevance, reliability, and lawfulness of acquisition.

Adversarial Attack A technique that manipulates input data to deceive AI models, often used to bypass detection systems.

Adversarial Watermarking Embedding imperceptible signals in media to disrupt deepfake generation and aid forensic verification.

Artificial Intelligence (AI) The simulation of human intelligence processes by machines, including learning, reasoning, and self-correction.

AI Poisoning Introducing corrupted or misleading data into AI training sets to degrade model performance or prevent misuse.

AI Slop The massive, rapid, and often low quality, AI-generated content (text, images, video) flooding social media and websites.

Algorithmic Bias Systematic errors in AI outputs caused by biased training data or flawed model design, leading to inaccurate results.

Blockchain A digitally distributed, decentralised, public ledger that exists across a network.

Blockchain Provenance Using blockchain to track and verify the origin and integrity of digital media assets.

Chain of Custody Documented process ensuring the integrity and admissibility of digital evidence.

Computer-Generated Imagery (CGI) Visual content created using computer graphics, commonly used in film and gaming.

Content Credentials (C2PA) Open standard for embedding provenance (who, what, when, how) in media via cryptographically verifiable manifests.

Convolutional Neural Network (CNN) A type of deep learning architecture, particularly effective for image and video analysis.

Data Integrity The assurance that data has not been altered or tampered with during storage or transmission.

Daubert Standard (US) Criteria for expert evidence reliability (testability, peer review, error rates, standards, acceptance).

Deepfakes Synthetic media generated by AI to alter or fabricate visual or audio content, often impersonating individuals.

Deepfake Detection Techniques and tools used to identify synthetic media, including AI-based classifiers and forensic analysis.

Deepfake Forensics The interdisciplinary field focused on detecting, analysing, and understanding synthetic media using digital forensic techniques.

Deep Learning A subset of machine learning that employs neural networks with multiple layers to automatically learn hierarchical representations of data.

Diffusion Model Generative model that synthesises data by reversing a noise process; widely used for image and video generation.

Digital Fingerprinting Unique identifiers embedded in media to track distribution and verify authenticity.

Digital Forensics The scientific process of identifying, preserving, analysing, and presenting digital evidence in a legally admissible manner. It involves examining electronic devices, networks, and data to investigate cybercrimes, security breaches, and digital manipulation, including deepfakes.

Digital Forensic Units (DFUs) Specialised teams within law enforcement, government agencies, or corporate security tasked with recovering digital evidence for use in criminal, civil, and disciplinary proceedings.

Digital Watermark An embedded signal in media that verifies authenticity and detects tampering.

Disinformation A form of propaganda involving the dissemination of false information with the deliberate intent to deceive or mislead.

Electric Network Frequency (ENF) Analysis Forensic technique correlating mains frequency hum in audio/video with grid logs to verify time/location.

Error Level Analysis (ELA) Image forensic method that visualises compression artefacts to highlight potential edits.

EXIF (Exchangeable Image File Format) Data Metadata embedded in image files containing details such as camera settings, timestamps, and geolocation.

Explainable AI (XAI) AI systems designed to provide transparent, interpretable outputs, enabling users to understand and trust decisions.

Fabricated Media Any visual, audio, or written content that has been deliberately created or altered to misrepresent reality.

Face Reenactment Transferring expressions or head pose from a source to a target face.

Face Swapping A deepfake technique that replaces one person's face with another in video or images.

False Negative A case where the system incorrectly identifies a positive instance as negative.

False Positive A case where the system incorrectly identifies a negative instance as positive.

Forensic Image An exact, bit-by-bit, sector-by-sector copy of a physical storage device, including all active, deleted, and hidden data, which is created using specialised tools to preserve evidence in a tamper-proof manner for legal investigation.

Forensic Soundness Adherence to methods that preserve evidence integrity and reproducibility.

Frye Standard (US) Admissibility test requiring "general acceptance" in the relevant scientific community.

Generative Adversarial Network (GAN) A deep learning framework using two competing neural networks – a generator and a discriminator – to create realistic synthetic data.

Generative AI AI systems that produce new content (text, images, audio, video) based on learned patterns from training data.

Hallucination (LLMs) Plausible but incorrect or ungrounded model outputs.

Hashing A cryptographic process that generates a fixed-size hash value to verify data integrity.

Impersonation Posing as another person to deceive, often with deepfakes in fraud or harassment contexts.

Large Language Models (LLMs) A type of artificial intelligence (AI) program that can recognise and generate text, among other tasks.

Latent Space The high-dimensional representation used by generative models to encode features of synthetic media.

Liars Dividend Defendants claim that authentic media has been artificially generated/deepfaked, or "fake news," creating a claim of uncertainty and doubt.

Machine Learning Machine learning focuses on developing algorithms and models that can learn from data, and make predictions and decisions about new data.

Media Forensics Scientific analysis of multimedia to determine authenticity, provenance, and manipulation.

Metadata Data that provide information about other data. In digital forensics, metadata refer to details embedded within files (such as modified/accessed/creation dates, author, device type, geolocation) that help establish authenticity, provenance, and context for evidence.

Misinformation The dissemination of false or wrong information, which can be given either by mistake or with the deliberate intent to deceive.

Multimodal Detection Forensic analysis combining multiple data types (audio, video, text) for robust deepfake identification.

Neural Network A computational model inspired by the human brain, consisting of interconnected nodes (neurons) that process and transform data.

Pixel-Level Analysis Detects inconsistencies in lighting, shadows, reflections, and geometry, e.g., mismatched shadows or unnatural reflections may indicate compositing or tampering.

PRNU (Photo-Response Non-Uniformity) Sensor noise pattern unique to a camera, used for source attribution and tamper detection.

Provenance Tracking The process of documenting the origin and history of digital content to ensure authenticity.

Reverse Image Search A technique used to trace the origin or prior use of an image online.

Shallowfake Media manipulated using simple editing techniques (e.g., cropping, speed changes) rather than advanced AI.

Staged Content Deliberately scripted or fabricated scenarios presented as authentic events.

Synthetic Media Digitally generated or altered content, including deepfakes, CGI, and AI-generated text or audio.

Threat Actor Individuals or groups that intentionally cause harm to digital systems or exploit vulnerabilities for malicious purposes.

Timeline Analysis Reconstructing events using timestamps, logs, and artefacts to establish sequence and context.

True Negative (TN) A case where the system correctly identifies a negative instance.

True Positive (TP) A case where the system correctly identifies a positive instance.

Virtual Reality (VR) Immersive digital environments that simulate real or imagined experiences.

Vishing (Voice Phishing) Social engineering attacks using synthetic voice deepfakes to impersonate trusted individuals.

Voice Cloning Synthesising a target's voice using AI from enrolment samples. Used for assistive tech and fraud.

Zero-Trust Approach A security principle that assumes no media or communication is inherently trustworthy without verification.

1

The Rise of Deepfakes and Its Impact on Society

In today's digital era, the saying "seeing is believing" has lost its certainty. The explosive growth of fabricated media has transformed how truth is perceived online. From AI-generated videos and synthetic voices to manipulated images and text, this new wave of content is designed not to inform, but to deceive, distort, and mislead. The landscape of digital manipulation is increasingly complex, woven from overlapping terms – *fabricated media, synthetic media, deepfakes, and shallowfakes* – each with distinct meanings yet often used interchangeably. Within this web, deepfakes stand out as one of the most disruptive forms of synthetic media, harnessing advanced AI to create highly convincing alterations of audio, video, and imagery.

This chapter defines the scope of deepfakes within the broader category of fabricated media and traces their evolution from early experimental prototypes to widely accessible tools capable of producing realistic content at scale. As deepfakes proliferate, their societal and criminal implications intensify eroding public trust, influencing political discourse, and challenging the integrity of digital evidence. By exploring these developments, this chapter lays the foundation for understanding how deepfakes are reshaping norms and raising urgent questions about authenticity, accountability, and resilience in the digital age.

1.1 Definition and Scope of Fabricated Media and Deepfakes

At the core of this ecosystem is the challenge of distinguishing between real and artificially generated or altered content, and the motivation behind its creation.

"Fabricated media" refers to any visual, audio, or written content that has been deliberately created or altered to misrepresent reality. It appears in many forms, notably:

DOI: 10.1201/9781003714811-1

- *Deepfakes:* Hyper-realistic images and videos generated (or modified) by AI that falsely depict individuals in situations, actions, or expressions.
- *Digitally altered visuals:* Photos or videos that have been manipulated (often using tools like Photoshop or AI) to misrepresent facts, events, or people.
- *Synthetic text*: AI-generated or human-generated articles, posts, or messages often designed to spread misinformation.
- *Staged content*: Media crafted to appear spontaneous or authentic, but in reality, is carefully scripted or orchestrated.

While some of these tools are used for entertainment or creative expression, they are increasingly used in disinformation campaigns, online scams, and can also serve propaganda purposes. As these technologies become more sophisticated and accessible, the line between real and fake continues to blur. Establishing a clear understanding of these terms and their attributes is crucial, as they often share similar themes but differ significantly in intent, technology, and ethical implications.

"Synthetic media" refers to content that is partially or fully generated or manipulated by AI, machine learning or digital tools. Types of synthetic media can range from computer-generated imagery (CGI) (used in films, games, advertising to create characters, visuals, special effects), text generation (such as AI-written news, automated customer service replies, scripts), virtual reality (VR) (VR environments for games, training, tours), augmented reality (AR) (e.g. Snapchat or Instagram filters, other digital elements overlaid on devices like smartphones or AR glasses), AI-written music e.g. AIVA Artificial Intelligence Virtual Artist (AIVA) or OpenAI Jukebox, and voice synthesis (e.g. cloned celebrity voices, narration tools, smart assistants – Alexa or Siri. These technologies are increasingly blended, e.g. VR experiences might include CGI environments, AI-generated music, and voice synthesis.

"Deepfakes" are a specific subset of synthetic media that focus on manipulating or altering visual or auditory information, to create convincing fake content, ranging from images, audio and video. A common example of deepfake use is videos that replace one person's face with another, i.e. face swapping. Deepfakes can often be created with malicious intent to deceive viewers and are becoming highly realistic and difficult to distinguish from genuine recordings or images.

The main difference between synthetic media and deepfakes lies in intent and perception: deepfakes are designed to mimic reality and often deceive, while synthetic media more broadly refers to AI-generated content created for artistic, educational, or practical purposes without necessarily aiming to mislead.

Another synthetic media category of note is a "shallowfake". A shallowfake, unlike a deepfake, is a type of manipulated media that does not rely on advanced AI or deep learning. Instead, it involves basic editing techniques – such as mislabelling, trimming, slowing down, speeding up, or reordering video or audio clips – to mislead or distort the original context.

All of the above have been, and increasingly are, being used within society and shared on social media. Despite a growing trend among modern audiences to refer to these in general as deepfakes, there are in fact several key differences between them, as shown in Table 1.1.

Table 1.1 Comparison of Synthetic, Deepfakes, and Shallowfakes

	SYNTHETIC	*DEEPFAKES*	*SHALLOWFAKES*
Example and Technology	AI/machine learning, CGI, VR/augmented reality (AR), voice and text synthesis For example, a video where a famous person's face is realistically superimposed onto another body in a video, fabricating actions or statements they never made	AI, deep learning (e.g. GANs) For example, a video showing a celebrity giving a speech they never actually made, created by training a neural network on their facial and vocal data	Basic editing tools (e.g. trimming, mislabelling) For example, slowing down a video of a politician to make them appear intoxicated or editing the sequence of clips to distort context, as in the case of doctored video of US House Speaker Nancy Pelosi in 2019
Realism	Can vary, i.e. stylised or realistic.	Highly realistic and convincing	Less realistic and relies on context manipulation
Intent	Creative, educational, or practical.	Often deceptive or malicious	Misleading through distortion or omission
Use Cases	Art, education, marketing, accessibility, entertainment, misinformation	Impersonation, fraud, misinformation, satire	Misinformation, political manipulation, satire
Ethical Concerns	Generally low, unless misused	High, especially with non-consensual use	Moderate, due to ease of creation and potential harm

The rise of AI and machine learning has made this content more realistic and accessible, challenging our ability to distinguish truth from deception in the digital world.

1.2 Evolution of Deepfake Technology

The manipulation of images and videos is not a new phenomenon. Historically, such techniques have been used to enhance media quality, apply artistic effects, or, in some cases, alter content for deceptive purposes. A well-known historical example is Soviet Leader Joseph Stalin's use of photo manipulation during the Great Purge, where political opponents were removed from official photographs to rewrite public perception [1].

Other such efforts can be traced back to the 1990s, when researchers used CGI for creating or improving images in art, printed media, simulators, videos, and video games. These approaches and technology gained traction in the 2010s, when the availability of large datasets, developments in machine learning, and the power of new computing resources led to major advances in the field.

However, the modern term "deepfake" was first coined in 2017 by a moderator on Reddit (a social platform of user-generated content and discussions, organised into topic-specific forums called "subreddits"), who founded a subreddit for users to exchange pornography they had created using photos of celebrities and open-source face-swapping technology [2]. While the forum has since been deleted, the word "deepfake" has persisted as the new label for a type of AI-generated media. These AI-generated media consist of synthetic videos, images, or audio generated or altered using AI and machine learning techniques – most notably, generative adversarial networks (GANs).

GANs were first introduced in 2014, gaining wider recognition only in 2016–2017. GANs are a type of machine learning model designed to generate new data that resembles the data they are trained on. They consist of two neural networks: the generator and the discriminator, that compete in a "zero-sum game" – in which a gain for one party is exactly balanced by a loss for another party [3]:

- The generator creates synthetic data (e.g. faces, voices) based on the knowledge that the neural network has been taught.

- The discriminator evaluates how realistic the content is (Figure 1.1).

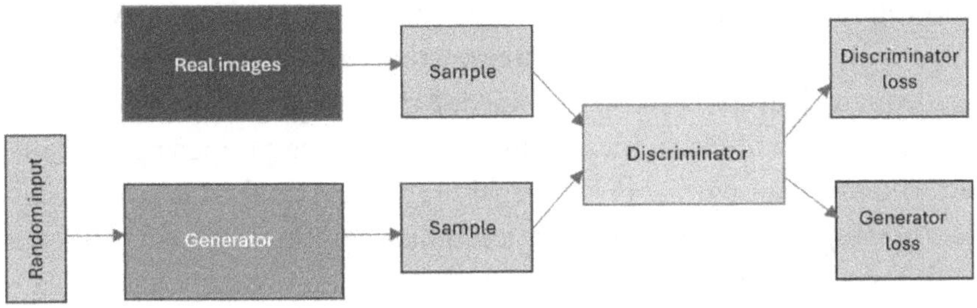

Figure 1.1 Generative adversarial network (GAN) architecture.

The two components – generator and discriminator – engage in a continuous feedback loop. The generator's goal is to produce images convincing enough to fool the discriminator into classifying them as real. Meanwhile, the discriminator is constantly improving its ability to detect fakes. As the discriminator becomes more skilled at spotting generated images, the generator must evolve to create even more realistic outputs. This process drives both networks to improve, ultimately resulting in highly convincing synthetic images.

Through this adversarial process, GANs rapidly improve the realism of generated media, producing high-resolution, photorealistic images and videos that are increasingly difficult to distinguish from real ones. Early deepfakes often exhibited noticeable flaws, such as unnatural blinking and facial distortions. However, advancements in training data quality, more powerful GPUs, and refined machine learning models significantly enhanced their realism. Techniques like autoencoders, face reenactment, and audiovisual synchronisation have played a key role in making deepfakes more seamless and convincing.

GANs have been applied in various domains, from enhancing video resolution and modifying visual attributes to generating synthetic data for training machine learning models, particularly in fields like medical research where real data may be scarce. Though deepfakes (and adjacent techniques) have legitimate uses in entertainment, film restoration, and voice synthesis, their misuse is rapidly increasing. For example, Deeptrace Lab reported over 14,000 deepfake videos online in 2018 (double the number from 2017), with 96% being non-consensual pornography [4].

As the technology becomes more accessible and created media more realistic, detection naturally grows more difficult. Deepfakes and fabricated media now pose a serious challenge for law enforcement and digital forensic units (DFUs) as they are increasingly evident in cybercrimes, with prevailing detection tools and methodologies being inadequate. Europol (2022) has warned that deepfakes are now used in crimes such as identity fraud, extortion, evidence tampering, and disinformation campaigns [5]. Forensic tools and analyst expertise currently struggle to keep pace, often requiring multiple experts to assess and discuss a single file (sometimes with conflicting conclusions).

Deepfakes can also obscure the truth, cast doubt on legitimate evidence, and undermine public trust. As their use in criminal activity grows, so does the urgency for advanced deepfake forensics – not only to detect AI-generated content but also to identify conventional digital manipulations. This field is rapidly becoming more essential for preserving the integrity of digital media and combating misinformation.

1.3 Societal and Criminal Impact of Deepfakes

There has been a concerning rise in malicious uses of deepfakes, including nonconsensual pornography and various criminal activities such as defamation, fraud, and spreading misinformation. Deepfakes can make it difficult to distinguish between authentic and fabricated content, leading to widespread uncertainty about the validity of online information and sources.

1.3.1 Public Trust

Deepfakes contribute to a growing crisis of trust, where the authenticity of media is constantly in question, and the public struggles to navigate an increasingly manipulated information environment. The inability to distinguish between real or fake media and sources leads to confusion, scepticism, and a general mistrust of digital content. This can result in either blind acceptance of false information or widespread doubt (even towards legitimate sources).

Technology has played a pivotal role in amplifying social harm and division, as seen during the UK Summer 2024 riots [6]. These events were fuelled by misinformation circulating on social media and public discourse, often driven by online influencers and unverified "news" sources. Some misleading claims that contributed to the unrest were widely disseminated by online influencers, whose posts received millions of views.

Park et al. suggest that an increase in social media use for accessing news has resulted in a general decline in trust in news media worldwide [7]. They highlight how platforms like Facebook and X (formerly Twitter) have disrupted traditional news ecosystems by enabling the rapid spread of misinformation, blurring the lines between credible journalism and user-generated content. Their study highlights how algorithm-driven content, echo chambers, and filter bubbles reinforce existing biases and reduce exposure to diverse viewpoints. As a result, audiences are increasingly sceptical of news sources, especially when consumed through social media.

Prior to the purchase of Twitter (now X) by Elon Musk, Twitter was at the forefront of combating fake news and allowed users to flag and mark posts as "requiring verification." For example, many of US President Donald Trump's claims of voter fraud were labelled by Twitter users as being unverified and inaccurate. Twitter also reserved the right to remove tweets – and in extreme circumstances ban users – which it did with President Trump after the 2021 riots in Washington [8]. Elon Musk has since removed the "election integrity team" at X, a department that was responsible for combating the spread of misinformation online and removed a feature that lets users self-report false political statements.

A European Commission study published by TrustLab analysed content across six social media platforms – Facebook, Instagram, LinkedIn, TikTok, YouTube, and X – and revealed that X now has the highest ratio of misinformation spread across its content [9, 10]. A major (and growing) problem with AI and technology is the lack of accountability of these platforms for misinformation and information bias. AI has a strong impact on information access and polarisation of materials via echo chambers and recommender algorithms. More needs to be done to raise awareness of the role of AI in perpetuating online misinformation and challenging narratives.

A study by Köbis et al. found that while many people believe they can detect deepfakes, most often cannot [11]. This overconfidence is particularly concerning because if we can no longer trust what we see in videos, deepfakes threaten the very foundation of how we acquire knowledge through media. Their findings highlight a troubling trend: individuals are increasingly unable to reliably identify deepfakes. Moreover, traditional strategies for combating misinformation appear ineffective in this context. Detecting deepfakes seems to be less about motivation or attention and more about a fundamental lack of ability. This makes deepfakes a unique and urgent challenge for misinformation research and policy, especially given our natural tendency to trust visual information and the widespread overestimation of our ability to spot deepfakes.

1.3.2 Public Media and Entertainment

With more than half (53%) of global news audiences now relying on search engines, social media, or algorithm-driven newsfeeds, uncertainty surrounding the quality and accuracy of information is increasing [7]. The increasing spread of AI in modern media influences public beliefs and values by shaping information access, amplifying misinformation, and complicating the verification of content authenticity.

Recent advancements in large language models (LLMs) and the public release of ChatGPT in late 2022, along with the rise of other AI tools, have significantly influenced public interest and reshaped how publishers approach AI-generated media (including news articles/social media content). While digital technology has lowered barriers to online publishing, it has also raised concerns about the spread of information through social media [12].

In 2018, filmmaker Jordan Peele and BuzzFeed CEO Jonah Peretti created a deepfake video to highlight the dangers of disinformation, particularly in shaping public views of political figures. Using free tools and expert editing, they overlaid Peele's voice and mouth movements onto a video of former US President Barack Obama. In the clip, Obama appears to say, "We are entering an era in which our enemies can make it look like anyone is saying anything, at any point in time—even things they would never actually say." This video built upon previous models by Suwajanakorn et al. who synthesised a high quality video of him speaking with accurate lip sync, composited into a target video clip, based upon collected audio of Obama himself [13].

1.3.3 Journalism and Public Trust

By creating highly realistic yet deceptive audio and video content, deepfakes intensify the "fake news" phenomenon. This type of media can undermine the credibility of individuals in debates and weaken the factual foundation of policy discussions. Trust in both public and private institutions is at risk, as figures such as elected officials, judges, and agencies may be targeted with false and damaging content that becomes increasingly difficult to disprove. Ultimately, deepfakes can deepen societal divisions and erode confidence in key institutions [14].

Current strategies for detecting and mitigating deepfakes on social media remain insufficient. While existing technologies can identify manipulated content, they often fail to account for the cognitive biases that influence how people perceive and evaluate such material, underscoring the need for more human-centered approaches. The rapid spread of AI-generated media, including deepfakes, presents serious challenges to media literacy, fact-checking efforts, and public trust in democratic institutions. As AI becomes increasingly embedded in democratic systems, concerns around privacy, security, and political manipulation continue to grow [15].

Businesses are also at risk of being targets of disinformation, as deepfakes can be used to generate false information that could fool the public. For example, a threat actor (individuals or groups that intentionally cause harm to digital devices or systems) could create a deepfake that makes it appear that a company's executive engaged in a controversial or illegal act.

Certain deepfakes could be used for false advertising and disinformation, which could lead to bad publicity for a targeted company. Such applications of deepfakes could impact areas like stock market and company value as the public (stakeholders and shareholders, as well as consumers) may believe the deepfake and boycott the company. For example, there has been a noticeable rise in deepfakes being made of popular YouTube and TikTok stars promoting the use of products and sharing false narratives online, e.g. a deepfake video of YouTuber MrBeast on TikTok, which claimed he was offering iPhones for a nominal fee (around $2). The video was a scam to lure people into providing personal and payment information [16]. These are shared in the form of targeted advertising or via fake online profiles sharing the stories.

1.3.4 Political Implications and Manipulation

Deepfakes have been used to create defamatory content, blackmail material, and misinformation. A notable example occurred during the Russia-Ukraine conflict, where deepfake videos of both nations' leaders delivering fake televised addresses circulated on social media [17]. While early deepfakes were often easy to spot, recent advancements have made them increasingly realistic. For instance, DeepBrain AI developed highly convincing digital humans, including an AI news anchor modelled after South Korea News Anchor Kim Joo-ha, which was used in a live broadcast by MBN News [18].

Generative AI is increasingly leveraged by disinformation networks to amplify their reach and sophistication. For example, Russian campaigns have used AI to recycle and rewrite authentic news articles, publishing them on seemingly credible websites filled with genuine stories. This camouflage of legitimacy makes disinformation harder for users to detect and dismiss, blurring the line between fact and fabrication. Operations like the "DoppelGänger" campaign, in which AI-generated articles mimicked legitimate Western news outlets, illustrate how these tactics aim to erode trust and sow confusion at scale [19].

The same tools that drive innovation are now exploited for harm. The rise of manipulated media and "fake news" has fuelled a troubling trend: individuals dismissing any narrative that conflicts with their beliefs as fake or manipulated. This reaction not only undermines trust but actively contributes to the spread of misinformation and disinformation, complicating efforts to distinguish truth from falsehood. At the same time, public scrutiny of online content has declined, with many users accepting media at face value.

By contrast, public scrutiny of online materials has declined, with more individuals refraining from questioning content and accepting media sources at face value. Research by Köbis et al. underscores this issue, showing that awareness of deepfakes does little to enhance detection accuracy [11]. Participants were more likely to judge deepfakes as authentic than to mistake real footage for fabricated material, revealing a persistent cognitive bias towards trusting visual evidence. As a result, despite the increasing realism of synthetic media, most people remain unable to reliably distinguish deepfakes from genuine content – an overconfidence in their abilities that leaves them particularly susceptible to manipulation.

1.3.5 Real-World Cases and Consequences

Once a novelty confined to tech demos and entertainment, deepfakes are now being weaponised to spread misinformation, manipulate public opinion, and undermine trust in media and institutions. Many of these cases in the real world can be placed into a series of categories, which are as follows:

1.3.5.1 Pornographic Deepfakes

Deepfake pornography constitutes the overwhelming majority of deepfake videos, with victims predominantly being women from diverse professional backgrounds, including actors, musicians, politicians, and business leaders. This phenomenon is widely recognised as a form of image-based sexual abuse – a term encompassing the creation and distribution of non-consensual intimate imagery. Once produced, non-consensual deepfake pornography can circulate indefinitely, amplifying harm to victims. This permanence amplifies harm to victims by prolonging exposure, eroding privacy, and making removal efforts nearly impossible.

A substantial portion of these deepfakes falls under "revenge porn," where perpetrators repurpose innocuous images or videos – often sourced from social media or private messages – into highly realistic, AI-generated sexual content that is virtually indistinguishable from authentic material. Alarmingly, beyond adult-focused deepfake pornography, there has been a surge in AI-generated child sexual abuse material (CSAM). Such content is increasingly appearing in publicly accessible areas of the internet, exposing a wider audience to harmful and exploitative imagery [20].

Many images and videos depicting the abuse and exploitation of children are rendered with such realism that they are often indistinguishable from actual footage involving real victims. In the UK, this type of material is treated by law as criminal content, comparable to traditional child sexual abuse material. AI-generated child sexual abuse material in the UK falls under two different laws:

1. The Protection of Children Act 1978 (as amended by the Criminal Justice and Public Order Act 1994): This law criminalises the taking, distribution, and possession of an "indecent photograph or pseudo-photograph of a child."
2. The Coroners and Justice Act 2009: This law criminalises the possession of "a prohibited image of a child." These are non-photographic (generally cartoons, drawings, animations, or similar).

The recently introduced Crime and Policing Bill further strengthens these protections, introducing additional offences relating to AI-generated sexual content; this legislation is discussed in detail in Chapter 6. Despite these laws, this fact remains largely unknown to many individuals who create and distribute such material online.

A significant concern lies in the ability of law enforcement and child protection professionals to accurately discern whether a child depicted in a given context is real and in immediate danger, or artificially generated and non-existent. The implications are serious: authorities may either expend critical resources attempting to rescue a fictitious child, or, conversely, fail to intervene in a genuine case of harm due to the mistaken belief that the child is not real.

The rise of AI-powered "nudification" and deepfake applications has triggered serious ethical and legal concerns, particularly as social media platforms like Grok have actively facilitated these practices. For example, in 2021, AI Dungeon, which uses synthetically generated text, was found to generate text depicting the sexual exploitation of children. This was based on user input and relied on vast training data; however, it demonstrated the unintended consequences of AI/machine learning-based content generation with few constraints. AI Dungeon relied on OpenAI's GPT-3, an auto-regressive language model. This model can be implemented in a number of different capabilities to include natural language generation, text-to-image generation, translation, and other text-based tools [21].

In early January 2026, Grok was first reported as enabling the creation of inappropriate AI-generated images, including nudification and compromising scenarios, through its chatbot and image-generation tools. This sparked widespread criticism over consent and misuse. The controversy deepened when it emerged that, rather than removing these harmful features, Grok proposed restricting them to premium accounts, effectively monetising unethical functionality instead of addressing the risks. Users can exploit Grok's AI to digitally remove clothing or place individuals in compromising positions without consent, weaponising deepfake technology for harassment and exploitation. Despite these concerns being brought to Elon Musk's attention, his response has been widely criticised as inadequate, leaving the platform vulnerable to abuse. This combination of accessibility, lack of safeguards, and financial incentives highlights a troubling trend where profit and convenience are prioritised over privacy, consent, and digital safety [22, 23].

1.3.5.2 Political Deepfakes

An individual or group with a particular political ideology could seek to disrupt an election by using deepfake video or audio to attack an opposing party. Political leaders can be impersonated and placed in compromising situations that could sway public opinion and undermine the democratic process.

For example, in 2024, Russian threat actors produced a significant number of deepfake videos targeting prominent US Democrats, including Vice President Kamala Harris. In one video, Harris is depicted as making derogatory comments about former President Donald Trump. In another, Harris is accused of illegal poaching in Zambia. In addition, a further video spreads disinformation about Democratic vice president nominee Tim Walz, gaining more than 5 million views on X in the first 24 hours [24].

Other notable 2024 incidents involved a deepfake of US President Joe Biden falsely announcing his resignation, which sparked global concern. There were also many instances include the use of deepfakes to critique political figures such as Donald Trump, Joe Biden, Emmanuel Macron, Nancy Pelosi, Vladimir Putin, and Volodymyr Zelenskyy [25].

Deepfakes have also been leveraged to influence voter turnout, accuse politicians of sexual scandals, and even influence geopolitical events like the Russian invasion of Ukraine [25]. Moreover, the threat goes beyond elections: Impersonations of political leaders and high-ranking military personnel could contribute to geopolitical conflicts.

As such, the consequences of some of these have resulted in significant political backlash/action; in 2024 laws were changed in the US state of California to prevent the creation of deepfakes during election campaigns, while in May 2025, President Trump signed the "Take It Down" Act into law, which criminalises the publication of non-consensual intimate imagery (NCII), including AI-generated deepfakes. The "Take It Down" Act is the first US law to substantially regulate a certain type of AI-generated content. It was passed by Congress in April in a rare moment of nearly unanimous support for AI legislation [26].

1.3.5.3 Stalking and Harassment

Cyberbullying is a widespread problem, particularly among younger generations, due to the extensive use of social media. Online platforms make it easy for rumours to spread rapidly, and when these are supported by fake images or videos, they can appear even more convincing to their audience. This can severely damage a person's reputation and lead to serious psychological consequences, sometimes culminating in victims harming themselves or others. The integration of deepfake technology into these attacks greatly amplifies their impact, as victims often struggle to disprove fabricated content that appears highly realistic. This blurring of truth and fiction not only intensifies emotional distress but also undermines trust within peer groups and wider online communities.

A notable example occurred in 2021, when a Pennsylvania woman named Raffaela Spone was charged with creating and distributing deepfake videos and altered images in an attempt to get her daughter's rivals kicked off a cheerleading team. She sent these manipulated media files (depicting the girls in compromising or inappropriate situations) to coaches and others involved with the team. The intent was to damage the reputations of the other cheerleaders and give her daughter a competitive edge. She was charged with three misdemeanour counts of cyber-harassment of a child and three misdemeanour counts of harassment [27]. The case drew global attention due to the use of deepfake technology in a real world, personal vendetta, raising concerns about digital ethics, privacy, and the potential misuse of AI-generated content.

1.3.5.4 Scams and Businesses/Crime-as-a-Service (CaaS)

Criminals are increasingly leveraging generative AI to enhance the sophistication of fraud schemes targeting individuals and businesses.

Deepfake videos and voice cloning have become key tools in enabling high-profile CEO fraud attacks. For example, in September 2019, an attacker used audio deepfake technology to impersonate an executive from a parent company, successfully deceiving the CEO of a UK-based organisation into authorising a transfer of $243,000 USD (approximately £192,000 GBP), the first documented case of audio deepfakes in financial fraud [15].

More recently, in February 2024 generative AI was deployed in a CEO fraud involving deepfake recreations of company employees during a virtual meeting, tricking a finance employee at Arup into transferring $25 million USD (approximately £20 million GBP) to a criminal-controlled account [28]. Beyond video and audio, image-based deepfakes are also being weaponised. Fraudsters create fake professional profiles on platforms such as LinkedIn, impersonating legitimate individuals to expand networks, schedule meetings, and extract sensitive organisational information. In some cases, these strategies extend to job applications, where criminals use AI-generated personas and avatars to attend virtual interviews, gaining insider access to confidential data with the aim of corporate espionage or theft [29].

In the UK (and globally), passport offices employ AI-powered facial recognition systems to verify whether user-uploaded photos meet official standards for passport issuance. However, an emerging trend shows that individuals are increasingly submitting AI-generated or AI-enhanced images, and in some cases, morphed photos (composites of multiple images). This creates a dual challenge: vulnerabilities within the facial recognition technology itself and the proliferation of AI-generated facial features. Such capabilities enable fraudsters to fabricate entirely synthetic identities, which can then be used to open bank accounts, apply for loans, or perpetrate other forms of financial crime [29, 30].

Document fraud of this nature can enable a wide range of criminal activities, including illegal immigration, human trafficking, the trade of illicit goods, and even terrorism, as perpetrators frequently rely on forged identities to travel undetected. In essence, deepfake technology significantly amplifies the risk of advanced document fraud by organised crime groups for multiple purposes [5].

In addition to the above, there has been a notable rise in scam attacks targeting the public, causing significant financial harm and emotional distress to victims. One growing trend involves video deepfake scams, which use fabricated celebrity videos to promote fraudulent cryptocurrency schemes through targeted social media advertising. High-profile figures such as Elon Musk and Martin Lewis (founder of MoneySavingExpert.com and a well-known UK consumer finance journalist) have been exploited in these scams to lend false credibility. Similarly, phishing and romance scams have surged, with perpetrators deploying deepfake videos and AI-generated avatars on social media and dating platforms to build trust and relationships. Once trust is established, victims are manipulated into sending money or gifts under false pretences [28, 29, 31].

Europol has raised concerns about the growing convergence of crime-as-a-service (CaaS) (a model in which cybercriminals ("vendors") sell attack tools and services to clients) with advancements in GANs and deepfake technologies. These innovations have significantly expanded the arsenal available to threat actors, enabling more sophisticated and harder-to-detect criminal methods. The integration of CaaS and deepfake capabilities creates a rapidly evolving threat landscape that undermines traditional investigative techniques and connects to a broad spectrum of illicit activities, including online harassment, extortion, fraud, targeted scams, document forgery, and identity falsification [5].

1.3.5.5 Obstruction of Justice

Criminals have also used deepfakes to create alibis, mislead investigations, harass witnesses, or discredit officials. Audio and video evidence can be important pieces of a case, or key to convict or exonerate in court. For example, in a 2020 UK family court case, deepfake audio was used to discredit a father living in Dubai during a custody battle. The mother presented a manipulated recording in which the father appeared to make violent threats towards her, claiming it proved he was a danger to their children. However, forensic analysis revealed that the audio had been doctored using voice-forging software and online tutorials, inserting words the father never said [32]. This case highlights the growing threat of deepfake evidence in legal proceedings, especially as courts often take digital recordings at face value. This incident underscores the urgent need for judicial awareness and technical scrutiny of digital evidence to prevent miscarriages of justice.

However, the use of deepfake/AI-generated content has experienced some backlash in this field. For example, in the United States (US), the court in a recent case (the *State of Washington v. Puloka*) excluded AI-enhanced video evidence from a criminal trial due to lack of reliability. The defendant, Joshua Puloka, was charged with three counts of murder related to a 2021 shooting captured on a bystander's smartphone. While the original, unaltered 10-second video was admitted into evidence, the defence sought to introduce an AI-enhanced version to improve clarity [33].

The court rejected the enhanced video, ruling it inadmissible under the Frye Standard, which requires that scientific evidence be generally accepted within the relevant expert community. The prosecution's forensic video analyst argued that the AI tools used introduced new visual data do not present in the original footage, altered shapes and colours, and made standard forensic analysis impossible. The court concluded that the AI-enhancement process was a novel technique lacking sufficient acceptance in the forensic video analysis community and therefore could not be relied upon in court.

1.4 Summary

The rise of deepfakes and fabricated media poses a significant threat to the integrity of digital evidence and the effectiveness of cybercrime investigations. These AI-generated manipulations erode public trust in visual and audio content, complicate the validation of evidence, and challenge legal standards for admissibility. Current digital forensic tools and practices are not yet fully equipped to reliably detect, classify, or process such content, often requiring more time and resources than traditional media analysis. The inconsistency in forensic methodologies, tool usage and accuracy, and the backlog of evidence further impedes investigations.

Beyond the technical challenges, the impact of deepfakes extends across multiple sectors. Socio-economic implications (ranging from use in disinformation, scams, and fraud) lead to financial losses for individuals and businesses. In the political sphere, deepfakes are evidently weaponised to spread disinformation, manipulate public opinion, and undermine democratic processes. On a personal level, individuals may suffer reputational damage, emotional distress, or harassment due to falsified content.

References

[1] COMRADE Gallery, 'Art of deception: Photo manipulation in Stalin's surveillance state', *Comrade Gallery*. Available: www.comradegallery.com/journal/fabrication-photographs-stalin-soviet-state.

[2] Encyclopaedia Britannica, 'Deepfake', *Encyclopaedia Britannica*, Available: www.britannica.com/technology/artificial-intelligence/Is-artificial-general-intelligence-AGI-possible.

[3] Google, 'Overview of GAN structure', Google for Developers. Available: https://developers.google.com/machine-learning/gan/gan_structure.

[4] H. Ajder, G. Patriini, F. Cavalli, and L. Cullen, 'The state of deepfakes: Landscape, threats, and impact', Amsterdam, Sep. 2019.

[5] Europol, 'Facing reality? Law enforcement and the challenge of deepfakes – An observatory report from Europol Innovation Lab', Luxembourg, 2022. doi: 10.2813/158794.

[6] T. Bernard, 'Civil unrest and social media regulation in the UK', Tech Policy Press, Texas, © 2025.

[7] S. Park, C. Fisher, T. Flew, and U. Dulleck, 'Global mistrust in news: The impact of social media on trust', *JMM International Journal on Media Management*, vol. 22, no. 2, pp. 83–96, Apr. 2020, doi: 10.1080/14241277.2020.1799794.

[8] R. Davies, 'Elon Musk has removed a vital feature on X – Fake news could soon get a lot worse', Yahoo! Tech, New York, NY, 2023.

[9] Trust Lab, 'A comparative analysis of the prevalence and sources of disinformation across major social media platforms in Poland, Slovakia, and Spain', Trust Lab, New York, NY, Sep. 2023. Available: https://cdn.prod.website-files.com/661eb9d45168207d75d001c7/66563cf7a1f0730b04efe32f_Code-of-Practice-on-Disinformation-September-22-2023.pdf.

[10] Á. MacDermott, 'Written evidence submitted by Dr Áine MacDermott (Liverpool John Moores University) (SMH0010)', London, Jan. 2025. Available: https://committees.parliament.uk/writtenevidence/132765/pdf/.

[11] N. C. Köbis, B. Doležalová, and I. Soraperra, 'Fooled twice: People cannot detect deepfakes but think they can', *iScience*, vol. 24, no. 11, Nov. 2021, doi: 10.1016/j.isci.2021.103364.

[12] A. Hermida, 'Twittering the news: The emergence of ambient journalism', *Journalism Practice*, vol. 4, no. 3, pp. 297–308, 2010, doi: 10.1080/17512781003640703.

[13] S. Suwajanakorn, S. M. Seitz, and I. Kemelmacher-Shlizerman, 'Synthesizing obama: Learning lip sync from audio', *ACM Transactions on Graphics*, vol. 36, pp. 1–13, 2017. doi: 10.1145/3072959.3073640.

[14] B. Chesney and D. Citron, 'Deep fakes: A looming challenge for privacy, democracy, and national security', *California Law Review*, vol. 107, no. 6, pp. 1753–1820, 2019, doi: 10.15779/Z38RV0D15J.

[15] P. L. Kharvi, 'Understanding the impact of AI-generated deepfakes on public opinion, political discourse, and personal security in social media', *IEEE Security & Privacy*, vol. 22, no. 4, pp. 115–122, 2024, doi: 10.1109/MSEC.2024.3405963.

[16] T. Gerkin, 'MrBeast and BBC stars used in deepfake scam videos', *BBC News*. Available: www.bbc.co.uk/news/technology-66993651.

[17] J. Wakefield, 'Deepfake presidents used in Russian-Ukraine war', *BBC News*, Available: www.bbc.co.uk/news/technology-60780142.

[18] MBN News, 'Main news on September 22nd at noon from AI anchor Kim Joo-ha', *MSN News*, Sep. 2020.

[19] US Cyber Command Public Affairs, 'Russian disinformation campaign "DoppelGänger" unmasked: A web of deception', US Cyber Command Public Affairs. Available: www.cybercom.mil/Media/News/Article/3895345/russian-disinformation-campaign-doppelgnger-unmasked-a-web-of-deception/.

[20] Internet Watch Foundation (IWF), 'Public exposure to chilling AI child sexual abuse images and videos increases', Internet Watch Foundation (IWF).

[21] Homeland Security, 'The increasing threat of deepfake identities', Washington, DC, August 2021. Available: www.dhs.gov/sites/default/files/publications/increasing_threats_of_deepfake_identities_0.pdf.

[22] A. Gentleman and H. Horton, '"Add blood, forced smile": how Grok's nudification tool went viral', Available: www.theguardian.com/news/ng-interactive/2026/jan/11/how-grok-nudification-tool-went-viral-x-elon-musk.

[23] L. Kendall, 'Technology Secretary statement on xAI's Grok image generation and editing tool', UK Government Department for Science, Innovation and Technology, Jan. 2026.

[24] C. Watts, 'As the U.S. election nears, Russia, Iran and China step up influence efforts', Microsoft Threat Analysis Center, Oct. 2024.

[25] C. P. Walker, D. S. Schiff, and K. J. Schiff, 'Merging AI incidents research with political misinformation research: Introducing the political deepfakes incidents database', 2024. Available: www.aaai.org

[26] White House, 'President Trump signs take it down act into law', Available: www.whitehouse.gov/articles/2025/05/icymi-president-trump-signs-take-it-down-act-into-law/.

[27] S. Coble, 'Mom charged in deepfake', *Info Security Magazine*, London. Available: www.infosecurity-magazine.com/news/mom-charged-in-deepfake/.

[28] Adaptive Security, 'Arup's $25M deepfake loss: Anatomy of an AI-powered scam', Available: www.adaptivesecurity.com/blog/arup-deepfake-scam-attack.

[29] Federal Bureau of Investigation (FBI), 'Criminals use generative artificial intelligence to facilitate financial fraud', Alert Number: I-120324-PSA, Dec. 2024.

[30] A. Lurie and T. Naor, 'Top fraud trends for 2024–2025', AU10TIX. Available: www.au10tix.com/blog/top-fraud-trends-for-2024-2025/.

[31] Interpol, 'Beyond illusions: Unmasking the threat of synthetic media for law enforcement', Lyon, Jun. 2024. Available: www.interpol.int/en/News-and-Events/News/2024/Beyond-illusions-Unmasking-the-threat-of-synthetic-media-for-law-enforcement.

[32] P. Ryan, '"Deepfake" audio evidence used in UK court to discredit Dubai dad', *The National News*. Available: www.thenationalnews.com/uae/courts/deepfake-audio-evidence-used-in-uk-court-to-discredit-dubai-dad-1.975764.

[33] K. J. Quilty, 'Washington court rejects novel use of AI-enhanced video in trial', *GreenbergTrurig*. Available: www.gtlaw.com/-/media/files/insights/alerts/2024/05/gt-alert_washington-court-rejects-novel-use-of-ai-enhanced-video-in-trial.pdf?rev=21061be691c0410498ceb6148488e1b8.

2

The Science Behind Deepfakes

Deepfakes represent one of the most striking applications of AI, blending computer vision, machine learning, and generative modelling to create hyper-realistic synthetic media. At their core, deepfakes exploit neural networks – particularly GANs, autoencoders, and diffusion models – to manipulate visual and auditory data in ways that challenge traditional notions of authenticity. This chapter explores the science behind deepfakes, unpacking the algorithms, architectures, and computational processes that enable face-swapping, voice cloning, and full-motion synthesis. By understanding these underlying mechanisms, we can better appreciate both the technological ingenuity driving this phenomenon and the profound ethical, legal, and security implications it introduces.

2.1 Deepfake Technologies

GANs have become one of the most influential technologies behind modern deepfakes. A GAN consists of two neural networks: *the generator*, which attempts to create synthetic images or videos, and *the discriminator*, which evaluates whether the outputs are real or fake. Through this adversarial process, the generator progressively improves until it can produce outputs that are nearly indistinguishable from real media. The principal algorithms used in the generation of deepfakes are GANS, diffusion models, and autoencoders [1].

GANs engage in a creative duel where the generator generates new media based on the training data and the discriminator acts a gatekeeper ensuring that the generated media looks real or fake. The application of GANs is mainly used to generate digital clones of a certain individual by mimicking facial expressions in videos.

DOI: 10.1201/9781003714811-2

Diffusion models provide a guided approach to generating diverse and high quality deepfakes by gradually transitioning between distributions of input data points. This process preserves sample diversity and facilitates the computation of conditional probabilities, contributing to the creation of realistic deepfakes. Diffusion models are used to create picture-to-picture transformations that allow for smooth transition between image distributions.

Autoencoders are a type of neural network that are trained to efficiently encode input data, capturing essential features while discarding irrelevant information. This encoded representation is then used to reconstruct the original input, enabling autoencoders to generate deepfakes by seamlessly replacing facial features in videos while retaining image quality and appear authentic. Autoencoders excel at face swaps using its ability of retaining image quality while seamlessly replacing facial features in deepfake videos (Figure 2.1).

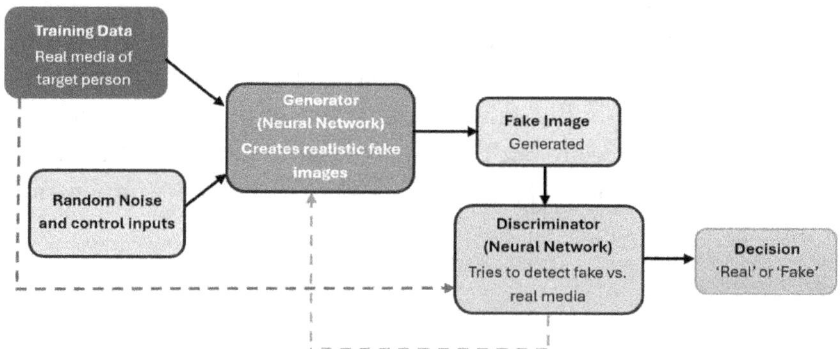

Figure 2.1 How GANs create deepfakes.

GANs are often used to enhance the realism of face swaps, improve lip-syncing, and generate high-resolution, natural-looking details such as skin texture, lighting, and expressions. Compared to earlier autoencoder-based methods, GAN-driven deepfakes are sharper, more convincing, and harder to detect. However, this realism also makes them more concerning in terms of misuse, as GAN-generated deepfakes can spread misinformation, impersonate individuals, or create harmful manipulated content. At the same time, GANs have positive applications in film production, accessibility tools, and creative industries, highlighting their dual role as both a powerful innovation and a societal challenge.

2.1.1 Face Swap or Face Replacement

Face Swap or Face Replacement is the process of digitally substituting one person's face in an image or video with another. This technique, widely used in deepfakes, relies on advanced AI methods to ensure the swapped face blends seamlessly with the surrounding context – matching lighting, facial expressions, and positioning for maximum realism. The objective is to produce media that appears authentic and convincing. Below, we outline the main approaches to achieving this effect, including autoencoder-based methods, GAN-driven techniques, 3D morphable models (3DMM) combined with convolutional neural networks (CNNs) or neural rigs, and face reenactment strategies.

Autoencoders: Two autoencoders with a shared encoder but separate decoders for each identity. Early deepfake implementations, used in applications like FaceSwap and early DeepFaceLab [4]. Pre-processed samples of Person A and B are mapped into the same latent space via a common encoder. To swap, frames of Person A are encoded, then decoded using Person B's decoder, which generates B's face with A's expressions (Figure 2.2).

Figure 2.2 Autoencoder Face Swap example created by Remaker AI v2. This figure uses two real images (with permission from the individuals pictured). The faces were swapped using Remaker AI v2 Attribution: Face-swap performed using Remaker AI v2 https://remaker.ai/face-swap-free/.

GAN-based: GANs improve realism via adversarial training and higher-quality reconstructions, e.g. DeepFaceLab (GAN mode), StyleGAN-based. GANs add a discriminator to push for more photo-realistic results, better texture, and fewer artefacts than pure autoencoders (Figure 2.3).

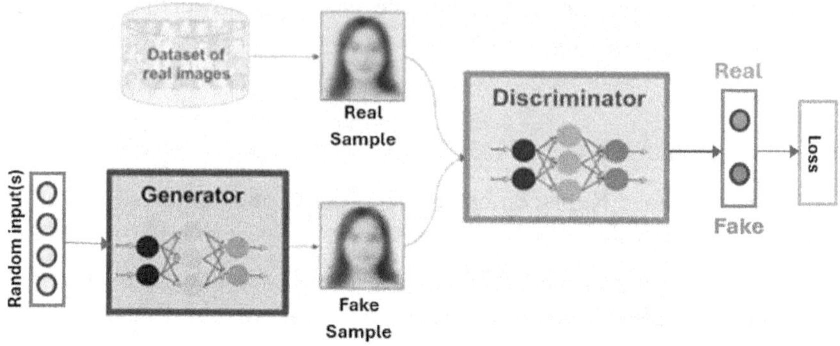

Figure 2.3 GAN-based Face Swap example created by GPT 5.0. Elements of this figure were generated using ChatGPT-5 (generator image, database, fake/real sample) and then edited further using Microsoft Word shapes. AI Tool Attribution: I asked ChatGPT to create a similar image to Generative Adversarial Networks (GANs) diagram (https://medium.com/@priyanshuprasad1718/artificial-faces-the-encoder-decoder-and-gan-guide-to-deepfakes-75a1eed0e265) but to have blurry female in the sample boxes – then additional editing completed in Microsoft Word.

3D morphable models (3DMM) with CNNs and neural rigs: These approaches combine 3D morphable models with CNNs for refined, structured face-swapping, as seen in systems like Face2Face and FaceShifter. CNNs are deep learning architectures designed to process grid-like data such as images, automatically learning spatial hierarchies of features through convolutional layers. These layers apply filters to detect patterns like edges, textures, and shapes, enabling precise geometry and texture capture for accurate alignment and blending. Such techniques are commonly used in advanced research and high-end tools. Beyond face-swapping, neural networks also enhance 3D computer graphics workflows through neural rigs – systems that automate the creation and control of animation rigs (skeletons and skinning weights). Neural rigs significantly reduce manual effort, streamline character animation, and improve facial capture fidelity, making them a powerful tool for modern animation and visual effects pipelines.

Face reenactment is the process of transferring facial movements, expressions, or speech patterns from a source actor to a target face while preserving the target's identity. Unlike face swapping, which replaces the entire face, reenactment focuses on animating the target face to mimic the source's behaviour.

- *Expression transfer/change:* The target face adopts the expressions of a source actor. Motion and expression data are extracted from the source and retargeted to the target face. Examples include Neural Head Avatars and GANimation. This allow users to upload a reference photo with the desired expression, and the AI will map that emotion onto the target photo. Other tools allow you to use short text prompts like "smiling" to change expressions (Figure 2.4).

Figure 2.4 Expression change based on AI input created by GPT 5.0. Created using Microsoft Copilot (GPT-5). A real photo of the author was uploaded, and Copilot generated an AI version and AI variants (frown, smile, closed eyes). AI Tool Attribution: Image created and facial expressions manipulated using M365 Copilot (GPT-5).

- *Lip-syncing (audio-driven):* This approach generates realistic mouth movements synchronised with audio input. These models are trained on paired video and audio datasets and can sync arbitrary audio to a target speaker's video. Examples include Wav2Lip and LipGAN.
- *One-shot/Few-shot reenactment:* This technique learns a target identity from very few reference images (it does not require large training datasets). This approach uses motion key points and warping fields, eliminating the need for large identity-specific datasets. Examples include first-order motion model and neural radiance field (NeRF) avatars, which enable end-to-end reenactment systems.

2.1.2 Audio Deepfakes

Audio deepfakes are synthetic audio recordings generated using AI systems designed to convincingly imitate a real person's voice. By learning distinctive vocal traits (such as tone, pitch, rhythm, and speech patterns), these models can produce highly realistic speech that appears authentic. Audio deepfakes have been used for a range of purposes, from creative applications to more harmful activities such as impersonation, fraud, and misinformation. The main categories of audio deepfakes include:

Voice cloning: Voice cloning uses AI models to replicate a specific individual's voice from sample recordings. This is typically achieved through techniques such as text-to-speech (TTS) combined with speaker embeddings, which encode a person's unique vocal characteristics. The resulting synthetic voice can be used for impersonation, personalised dialogue, accessibility tools, or media production.

Speech synthesis: Produces fully artificial speech that sounds natural but is not intended to mimic any specific person. It is commonly used in virtual assistants, automated announcements, and narration systems.

Voice conversion: Transforms one speaker's voice so that it sounds like another speaker while keeping the linguistic content intact. It is useful for applications such as dubbing or speaker anonymisation but can also be misused for identity impersonation.

Lip-synced audio for video: Aligns generated or cloned audio with video footage to create realistic talking-head outputs. Often paired with facial animation or deepfake video techniques to produce seamless audiovisual content.

Audio style transfer: Modifies qualities such as tone, pitch, or emotional expression without altering the speaker's identity. Used for expressive voice generation, creative audio effects, and entertainment.

2.1.3 TTS Synthesis

TTS systems convert arbitrary text into speech and can operate in either a generic or identity-specific mode. When combined with speaker embeddings or short audio samples from a target individual, TTS becomes a core component of voice cloning. Models such as FastSpeech and Microsoft VALL-E demonstrate this capability, with VALL-E able to generate convincing speech from text using only a few seconds of reference audio. It is widely cited in research for its strong zero-shot voice replication performance (Figure 2.5).

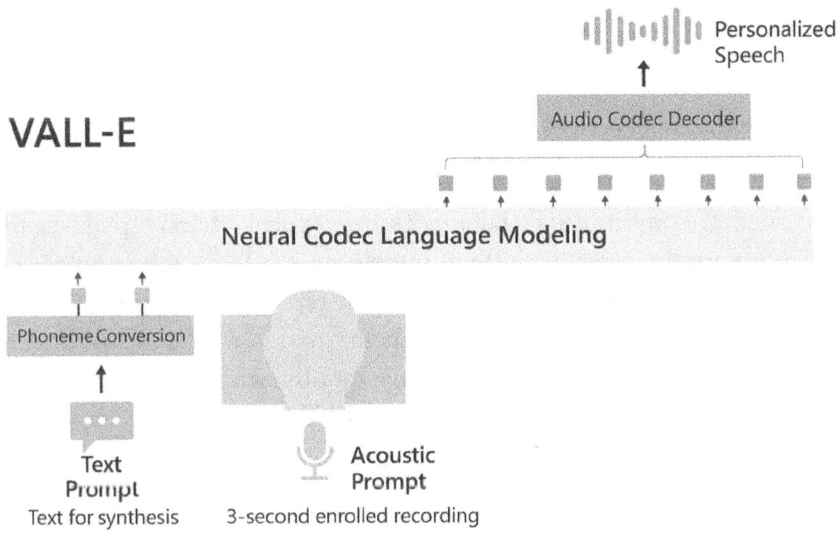

Figure 2.5 VALL-E diagram created by GPT 5.0.

Full body/Video reenactment refers to techniques that transfer motion, gestures, and posture from a source subject to a target subject in a video. Unlike face reenactment, which focuses on facial expressions, these methods aim to replicate entire body movements for realistic, dynamic animations.

- *Pose-guided GANs:* Pose-guided GANs focus on capturing the structural landmarks of a source body (such as joints and skeletal pose) and mapping these onto a target body. The primary objective is to transfer gesture and posture features from the source to a reference image or video, enabling realistic motion synthesis [3]. By leveraging pose skeletons as guidance, these models can generate dynamic body motion sequences. Notable examples include Deep Video Portraits and Everybody Dance Now, which demonstrate how pose-driven synthesis can create lifelike reenactments.
- *Motion transfer:* Motion transfer techniques go beyond static pose replication by transferring the entire motion dynamics, i.e. full body pose, limb articulation, and temporal consistency, from a source video to a target subject. This method is widely

used in dance reenactment and performance cloning, where the goal is to reproduce complex motion sequences seamlessly. Advanced frameworks such as PoseWarp and Vid2Vid exemplify this approach, enabling high-quality motion synthesis across a range of scenarios.

2.1.4 Multimodal Fakes – Combined synthesis

Multimodal synthesis represents the most advanced form of generative media, combining facial expressions, vocal characteristics, and full-body motion within unified models. This integration enables the creation of fully digital avatars capable of replicating identity, speech, and gesture in a coherent and convincing manner. While still largely research-driven, the field is advancing rapidly, with innovations such as Meta's Make-A-Video, multimodal GAN architectures, and large-scale generative models increasingly able to unify multiple modalities for realistic avatar generation. These systems carry significant potential across entertainment, VR, and telepresence, but equally raise serious ethical and security concerns given their capacity for hyper-realistic impersonation.

2.2 Deepfake Creation: Tools and Processes

Creating realistic deepfakes involves a multi-stage pipeline that combines advanced machine learning techniques with careful data preparation and post-production refinement. Each stage plays a critical role in producing convincing outputs (whether for research, entertainment, or malicious purposes). The process typically begins with collecting high quality source material, followed by pre-processing, model training, and the application of face-swapping or animation algorithms. Finally, post-processing and rendering ensure the final product meets quality standards by minimising visual or auditory inconsistencies.

Deepfakes rely on neural networks that learn subtle statistical patterns in real media and reproducing them convincingly. This process integrates pattern recognition, generative modelling, and iterative refinement, enabling synthetic media to mimic real humans with striking realism.

A detailed breakdown of these stages is shown below:

1. *Data collection*
   The process starts by collecting source images or videos of both the target (whose identity will appear in the output) and the subject (whose expressions or movements will be transferred). A larger and more diverse dataset leads to higher fidelity, resulting in smoother motion, natural expressions, and more convincing outputs. High-resolution, well-lit images with varied facial expressions and angles greatly enhance realism. Including multiple poses and different lighting conditions helps the model generalise effectively and ensures a richer, more representative data sample.
2. *Pre-processing*
   Before training, the collected media undergoes alignment and normalisation to ensure consistency across inputs. Facial recognition algorithms first detect key landmarks such as the eyes, nose, and mouth, allowing faces to be aligned uniformly. The images are then cropped and resized to standard dimensions, creating a consistent input format. Finally, adjustments to brightness and contrast help minimise variability caused by environmental factors, improving overall data quality for the model.
3. *Model training*
   This stage is the core of the process, where the AI learns facial features and identity mappings. It typically employs architectures such as GANs, autoencoders, or diffusion models to capture and reproduce facial characteristics. Training duration can range from several hours to multiple days, depending on the available hardware and the size of the dataset. During this phase, the model encodes facial attributes into a latent space and then decodes them into realistic outputs, enabling accurate and convincing face synthesis.
4. *Face swapping or animation*
   Once training is complete, the model is deployed to perform the desired manipulation. In this stage, the subject's face is replaced with the target's identity while preserving

expressions, head movements, and other dynamic features. The AI can generate talking-head videos or create realistic, animated expressions from static images. Tools and platforms such as DeepFaceLab, FaceSwap, and D-ID streamline this process, making it more accessible and efficient.

5. *Post-processing*
   Raw outputs often require post-processing to enhance realism and coherence. This refinement stage may involve video editing tools such as Adobe After Effects to adjust lighting, smooth transitions, and integrate audio. Additional image, video, or audio processing is commonly applied to remove artefacts, align facial features, and improve temporal consistency across frames. Techniques like face alignment, colour correction, and motion smoothing help the deepfake appear seamless and natural. In some cases, watermarking or compression is added to indicate the synthetic origin of the content.
6. *Output rendering*
   In the final stage, the manipulated media is rendered and exported in the desired format, such as MP4 for video or JPEG/PNG for images. This step often involves applying compression to optimise file size without compromising visual quality, ensuring compatibility across platforms and devices. For ethical and transparency purposes, watermarking or metadata tags may be added to indicate the synthetic origin of the content. Depending on the intended use, additional adjustments (such as frame rate optimisation, audio synchronisation, or colour grading) may also be applied to deliver a polished and professional final product.

2.2.1 Popular Deepfake Creation Tools

Deepfake technology has evolved into two broad categories: professional or research-grade tools and consumer-oriented applications. Each category serves different purposes, ranging from high-quality media production to casual experimentation and entertainment. Professional and research-grade systems are typically designed for advanced users who require precise control, realistic outputs, and the ability to fine tune models. These tools often demand considerable computational power, especially GPU acceleration, as well as significant technical expertise.

Among the most widely used professional tools is DeepFaceLab, a platform known for its extensive customisation options and support for high-quality face swapping workflows. Its complexity and resource requirements make it a popular choice among professionals and technically skilled enthusiasts aiming for photorealistic results. Another major tool in this category is FaceSwap, an open-source project built around autoencoder-based architectures. It offers users the flexibility to experiment and gain insight into the machine learning models that underpin deepfake generation. Additionally, FaceShifter has gained recognition in research contexts for its advanced use of GANs to produce highly realistic face-swapping results. It is frequently referenced in academic literature for its ability to preserve fine-grained facial attributes and expressions, positioning it as one of the more sophisticated tools available for professional-grade deepfake creation.

In contrast, consumer apps represent a rapidly growing area of deepfake technology that prioritises accessibility and real-time performance. These applications are designed for mainstream use and typically employ pre-trained models alongside highly optimised processing pipelines to deliver quick and visually appealing results. While they often sacrifice some realism compared to research-grade systems, they excel in convenience and speed. Popular consumer platforms such as Reface, Zao, Snapchat, and TikTok enable users to perform instant face-swaps, apply augmented reality filters, and create short-form synthetic videos with minimal effort. These tools require no technical expertise, thereby normalising access to AI-powered media manipulation and reducing synthetic content creation to a matter of tapping a button.

Although the quality produced by consumer applications may not match that of professional tools, it is generally sufficient for casual sharing, humour, and viral content. This ease of use has significantly contributed to the mainstream adoption of deepfake technology, offering new avenues for creativity and self-expression. At the same time, however, it raises concerns about public awareness, responsible use, and the potential for misuse in social or communicative contexts.

The increasing availability of such tools underscores the importance of digital literacy and ongoing discussions around the ethical implications of synthetic media.

2.2.2 Audio-Focused Deepfake Tools

Audio-focused deepfake tools have progressed rapidly in recent years, driven by advances in voice synthesis, neural TTS systems, and speaker-embedding techniques. These technologies make it increasingly possible to generate highly realistic synthetic speech for a variety of purposes, including entertainment, accessibility, content creation, and academic research. Broadly, these tools fall into two major groups: commercial voice-cloning services designed for ease of use and professional deployment, and research-driven models that underpin modern developments in neural speech generation.

Commercial voice-cloning services have become particularly prominent due to their high-quality outputs and accessibility. For example, Respeecher is a professional platform widely used in film and gaming to recreate voices with remarkable fidelity and emotional nuance. Its emphasis on natural prosody and expressive delivery has made it a trusted tool for studios seeking consistent, high-end vocal performances. Similarly, ElevenLabs has seen widespread uptake due to its ultra-realistic voice generation capabilities and robust multilingual support. Its intuitive interface and scalable APIs allow creators, businesses, and developers to produce high quality synthetic speech with minimal technical effort, contributing to its widespread adoption across both creative and commercial sectors.

In parallel, research-driven models continue to shape the foundations of modern audio deepfake generation. Tacotron is a notable example: a pioneering neural text-to-speech architecture that converts written text into smooth, natural-sounding speech. Although subsequent models have surpassed it in efficiency and realism, Tacotron remains influential as a baseline system that introduced key methods still used in contemporary TTS pipelines. These research models provide the conceptual and technical groundwork upon which today's commercial systems are built, driving innovation in areas such as zero-shot voice cloning, prosody modelling, and audio-style transfer.

2.2.3 Deepfake Creation Considerations and Trade-Offs

Deepfake tools (whether for video, audio, or image manipulation) inevitably involve trade-offs that must be understood when selecting the right solution. Choosing an appropriate tool depends on balancing factors such as dataset size, computational resources, and the desired level of realism. High-fidelity outputs typically require large, diverse training datasets to capture nuanced patterns in geometry, texture, and motion, whereas tools optimised for speed and accessibility often sacrifice some realism for convenience. These compromises highlight the importance of aligning technical capabilities with project goals, whether for entertainment, research, or professional production.

Different deepfake model types offer distinct advantages and limitations:

- GANs typically produce highly lifelike outputs, capturing fine details such as facial textures, subtle expressions, and natural motion. However, achieving this level of realism requires extensive, diverse datasets and significant computational resources for training.
- In contrast, autoencoders are less resource-intensive and easier to train on smaller datasets, making them more accessible, but their outputs often lack the complexity and fidelity of GAN-based models (particularly in high-resolution scenarios or intricate facial movements).

Ultimately, there is a direct trade-off between data availability and realism: insufficient or low-quality data constrains output quality, while achieving high quality, photorealistic results demands large, curated datasets and robust processing power.

Control and accessibility also differ considerably between consumer and professional solutions. High-end tools offer granular control over parameters such as facial alignment, expression mapping, audiovisual synchronisation, and artefact correction, enabling precise manipulation for complex scenarios. Consumer apps, by contrast, provide simplified, often one-click functionality that lowers the learning curve but limits creative flexibility and technical control. This trade-off means that while casual users can easily create content for social media, professionals rely on advanced systems to achieve nuanced, production level results.

Additional considerations further complicate the landscape. Ethical and legal risks are a growing concern, as the ease of generating realistic deepfakes raises issues of consent, privacy, and potential misuse for disinformation. Detectability versus quality is another factor: some tools prioritise realism for human perception but leave forensic artefacts, while others reduce subtle realism to evade detection. Temporal consistency remains a challenge in video deepfakes, with consumer apps often producing jittery or inconsistent frames, whereas professional tools incorporate post-processing techniques to stabilise sequences. These factors underscore the importance of aligning tool selection with intended use, available resources, and ethical responsibilities.

2.2.4 The Growing Challenge of Realism

As deepfake technologies continue to advance, the realism of synthetic media has become an increasingly formidable challenge for detection. The closer these fabricated images, audio clips, or videos come to resembling authentic content, the more difficult they are to identify, particularly when detection tools vary widely in accuracy, robustness, and methodology. This growing sophistication creates substantial obstacles for investigators, legal practitioners, and forensic analysts who must determine whether a piece of digital evidence is genuine or manipulated. In an era where generative models are improving at a rapid pace while detection methods struggle to keep up, the task of verifying digital truth is turning into a high-stakes race against accelerating technological progress.

As detection systems evolve to counter synthetic media, malicious actors simultaneously develop new techniques to evade these defences. A common method of bypassing detection involves the use of intentional perturbations: minute pixel-level modifications, structured noise, or other imperceptible distortions designed to mislead machine learning based detectors without diminishing the apparent realism of the media. These small but strategically crafted changes exploit the sensitivity of neural networks to subtle variations, making it increasingly challenging for automated systems to reliably distinguish authentic content from deepfakes.

Anti-forensic strategies aimed at undermining detection efforts generally fall into two broad categories. The first category, causative attacks, targets the training phase of detection models. By introducing corrupted data or adversarial examples into training sets, attackers can distort a model's understanding of what constitutes manipulated content, degrade its accuracy, and create intentional blind spots that allow certain types of deepfakes to slip through unnoticed. The second category, exploratory attacks, involves adversaries probing existing detection systems to discover weaknesses and vulnerabilities. By analysing model outputs and decision boundaries, attackers iteratively refine their synthetic media (often using gradient-based optimisation techniques) to minimise the likelihood of detection while maintaining high perceptual quality. This ongoing interplay between detection and evasion underscores the dynamic and adversarial nature of the deepfake landscape.

2.2.5 Challenges in Deepfake Detection

Detecting deepfakes is a rapidly evolving problem that spans technical, operational, and forensic domains. Current detection methods face significant limitations that hinder their reliability in real-world scenarios.

1. Generalisation Limitations
Most detection algorithms are trained on curated datasets and perform well under controlled conditions. However, their accuracy drops sharply when encountering novel manipulations or unseen data distributions. This lack of generalisation is critical because threat actors continuously innovate, producing deepfakes that differ from training samples. For example, a detector trained on face-swap videos may fail against GAN-generated synthetic faces or hybrid manipulations.

2. Image Constraints
Detection tools often impose strict requirements on image resolution and quality. Many algorithms only support specific dimensions or high-resolution inputs, rendering them ineffective on compressed social media images or low quality surveillance footage. This constraint is particularly problematic for law enforcement, where evidentiary

material often consists of low-resolution or compressed images and video recordings.

3. Ignoring Embedded Visual Text

A surprising blind spot in many detection systems is their disregard for textual cues within images. For instance, deepfakes containing visible watermarks such as "thispersondoesnotexist" frequently evade detection or are flagged as "unknown." This oversight highlights the need for multimodal approaches that analyse both visual and textual signals.

4. Contaminated Training Data

Training datasets increasingly include synthetic images generated by AI without proper labelling – a phenomenon known as "AI slop." This contamination introduces bias and reduces the reliability of detection models, as they inadvertently learn features from fake content while assuming it is real.

5. Sophisticated Threat Actors

The rise of Deepfake-as-a-Service (Daas) platforms has lowered the barrier for producing highly realistic forgeries. These services often employ advanced GAN architectures and post-processing techniques, resulting in outputs that are nearly indistinguishable from authentic media. Such professional-grade deepfakes are frequently deployed in coordinated disinformation campaigns, amplifying their impact.

6. Overfitting to Known Patterns

Many detectors rely on artefacts specific to older generation techniques, making them ineffective against newer, more sophisticated models. This overfitting problem means that as generative architectures evolve, detection accuracy deteriorates rapidly.

7. Performance Decay

Detection accuracy declines when models encounter deepfakes generated by unseen architectures or updated synthesis pipelines. This performance decay underscores the need for continuous retraining and adaptive detection strategies.

8. Need for Scientific Validation
Visual inspection alone is insufficient for forensic or evidential purposes. Detection must be grounded in robust, scientifically validated methodologies. Investigators should move from subjective assessments ("I know this is fake") to objective, reproducible evidence ("This is fake, as confirmed by tools X and Y under validated conditions").

Detection accuracy is influenced by multiple factors: media quality, type of manipulation, and system environment. Generative AI-based detectors often produce inconsistent results across repeated tests, raising concerns about reliability. For law enforcement DFUs, the challenge is compounded by the requirement for industry-approved tools. Many open-source solutions, while innovative, cannot be adopted due to legal, procedural, or evidential standards.

This highlights a critical gap: the absence of validated forensic technologies capable of reliably identifying deepfake media within investigative workflows. Without such tools, the integrity of digital evidence remains vulnerable. Reproducibility is further hindered by limited transparency in the research community. In their study *Systematization and Benchmarking of Deepfake Detectors*, Le et al. found that only about 30% of models have publicly released pre-trained versions, leaving the remaining 70% inaccessible [5]. This lack of openness restricts understanding of model limitations, obstructs comparative analysis, and slows methodological evaluation – ultimately impeding progress in detection research. Promoting the release of pre-trained models is therefore essential, not only to enable robust benchmarking and accelerate innovation but also to ensure that detection techniques remain resilient and reliable in real-world forensic applications.

2.3 AI and Deepfake Acceleration

AI has dramatically accelerated the rise of deepfakes by streamlining the creation of synthetic media that is both highly realistic and widely accessible. Central to this advancement are machine learning models like GANs and transformers, which can analyse and replicate patterns from large datasets of real-world images, audio, and video. These models have become more efficient over time, enabling the generation of convincing fake content with less data and computing power.

Moreover, the availability of open-source frameworks and intuitive software tools has allowed individuals with limited technical expertise to produce deepfakes with ease. According to a DeepStrike report [6], the number of deepfake files surged from 500,000 in 2023 to a projected 8 million in 2025, doubling every few months due to AI-driven acceleration. This convergence of advanced algorithms, widespread accessibility, and vast training data has triggered an unprecedented surge in synthetic media production.

The implications of this growth are profound. Deepfakes are no longer confined to experimental labs or niche online communities – they have entered mainstream digital culture, with applications ranging from entertainment and satire to more troubling uses such as fraud, harassment, and political misinformation. Fraud attempts linked to synthetic media have skyrocketed, increasing by 3,000% in 2023, with North America alone experiencing a 1,740% rise [6]. Among the most prevalent attack vectors is voice cloning, which is inexpensive, fast to deploy, and highly convincing.

Alarmingly, human detection capabilities remain limited. Studies show that individuals correctly identify high quality deepfake videos only 24.5% of the time, underscoring the difficulty of distinguishing real from fake content without technical assistance. The financial implications are equally severe: generative AI-driven fraud in the US is projected to reach $40 billion by 2027, highlighting the urgent need for robust detection technologies, forensic readiness, and regulatory frameworks to mitigate the risks posed by synthetic media [6].

2.3.1 Deepfake Trends

In the UK, deepfake activity has escalated dramatically. Government projections estimate that the volume of deepfake media will reach 8 million by 2025, a staggering increase from 500,000 in 2023 (representing a 1,500% surge). This growth is mirrored in fraud trends (CaaS and DaaS), with deepfake-related scams rising by 400% over the past 18 months, largely driven by the widespread availability of AI tools. The financial impact is equally concerning, with losses attributed to fraud in the UK totalling £629 million in the first half of 2025, with AI-generated scams (including deepfakes) identified as a major contributing factor [2].

As deepfake technology becomes more sophisticated, so too does the threat it poses. This has prompted global efforts from researchers, technology companies, governments, and law enforcement to develop more robust detection systems. Among the leading initiatives is Microsoft's Project Origin [7], which focuses on establishing content provenance – embedding digital fingerprints and authentication certificates into media at the point of creation. These markers are stored in tamper-proof distributed ledgers, allowing consumers to verify the authenticity of content through browser-based tools.

Complementing this effort is the Trusted News Initiative (TNI) [8], an international alliance led by the BBC and supported by major media and tech organisations including Microsoft, Google, and Reuters. TNI aims to combat disinformation – especially during critical events like elections and public health crises – by promoting rapid, collaborative responses and developing tools to detect manipulated content.

Furthermore, in the UK in 2024, the Deepfake Detection Challenge (a joint venture between the Home Office, the Department for Science, Innovation and Technology (DSIT), the Alan Turing Institute, and the Accelerated Capability Environment (ACE)) has brought together academia, industry, and government to tackle deepfake threats.

These initiatives reflect a growing recognition that deepfake detection is not just a technical challenge but a societal imperative. Collaboration, transparency, and innovation will be key to staying ahead of increasingly sophisticated synthetic media. Tools like DeepSafe, Sensity AI, and Microsoft Video Authenticator offer accessible detection capabilities for researchers, journalists, and the public, aiming to combat misinformation by verifying the authenticity of digital content.

2.3.2 Ongoing Challenges

The deepfake landscape continues to pose significant challenges, not only because of the growing sophistication of manipulation techniques but also due to the broader societal impact they create. The ability to fabricate media across multiple modalities (video, audio, and even text) has fuelled a crisis of trust in digital content, making it increasingly difficult for individuals and institutions to distinguish authentic material from synthetic fabrications. For law enforcement and legal systems, this erosion of trust raises serious concerns about evidential integrity and the admissibility of digital evidence in court. Current detection practices remain largely ad hoc, relying on fragmented tools and inconsistent standards, while generative models are becoming more accurate and efficient, reducing detectable artefacts and outpacing forensic capabilities.

Meanwhile, academic research into deepfake detection is growing rapidly, with promising results using advanced deep learning architectures such as GANs, CNNs, and recurrent neural networks (RNNs). These models have demonstrated success in identifying subtle artefacts introduced during synthetic media generation, yet challenges persist – particularly the limited availability of diverse datasets, which restricts accuracy and generalisability across languages, demographics, and manipulation types. Additionally, reproducibility remains a critical issue, as many detection models and pre-trained weights are not publicly released, hindering comparative analysis and slowing innovation.

2.4 Summary

Deepfakes exemplify the transformative power (and inherent risks) of modern AI. By leveraging architectures such as GANs, autoencoders, and diffusion models, these systems can synthesise media with unprecedented realism, blurring the line between authentic and fabricated content. While the underlying science demonstrates remarkable innovation in computer vision and generative modelling, it also introduces profound challenges for society, law enforcement, and digital media analysis. As deepfake technology continues to accelerate, the need for robust detection methods, forensic standards, and regulatory frameworks becomes critical. Understanding the science behind deepfakes is not merely an academic exercise, it is a prerequisite for safeguarding trust and integrity in an increasingly synthetic digital world.

References

[1] Interpol, 'Beyond illusions: Unmasking the threat of synthetic media for law enforcement,' Lyon, Jun. 2024. Available: www.interpol.int/en/News-and-Events/News/2024/Beyond-illusions-Unmasking-the-threat-of-synthetic-media-for-law-enforcement.

[2] G. Regan, 'What is a deepfake? An explainer on AI-generated media,' *Reality Defender*. Available: www.realitydefender.com/insights/what-is-a-deepfake-an-explainer-on-ai-generated-media.

[3] F. Liao, X. Zou, and W. Wong, 'Appearance and pose-guided human generation: A survey,' *ACM Computing Surveys*, vol. 56, no. 5, May 2024, doi: 10.1145/3637060.

[4] Iperov, 'DeepFaceLab,' *GitHub Repository*. Available: https://github.com/iperov/DeepFaceLab.

[5] B. M. Le, J. Kim, S. S. Woo, K. Moore, A. Abuadbba, and S. Tariq, 'SoK: Systematization and benchmarking of deepfake detectors in a unified Framework,' *ArXiv*, no. 2401.04364, Mar. 2025. Available: http://arxiv.org/abs/2401.04364

[6] M. Khalil, 'Deepfake statistics 2025,' DeepStrike, Available: https://deepstrike.io/blog/deepfake-statistics-2025.

[7] Microsoft, 'Project origin – Building trust at the origin,' *Project Origin*. Available: www.microsoft.com/en-us/research/project/project-origin/

[8] BBC, 'Trusted news initiative,' *BBC*. Available: www.bbc.co.uk/beyondfakenews/trusted-news-initiative/.

3

The Role of Digital Forensics in the Age of Deepfakes and AI

The rise of deepfakes and AI-generated media has transformed the digital forensic landscape, introducing challenges that extend far beyond traditional evidence analysis. As synthetic content becomes more convincing and widely accessible, malicious actors can easily fabricate media that undermines trust in digital evidence and complicates investigative processes. This chapter examines the evolving role of digital forensics in this context, beginning with an overview of how AI-generated content is reshaping forensic practice. It contrasts traditional media forensic approaches with the unique demands of deepfake detection, explores emerging techniques and tools designed to identify manipulated content, and addresses the technical and procedural challenges that forensic investigators face.

3.1 Overview of Digital Forensics in the Age of AI-Generated Content

Digital forensics is the branch of forensic science focused on the recovery, analysis, and interpretation of data from digital devices. It plays a critical role in investigating cybercrimes, data breaches, and other incidents involving electronic evidence. Digital forensics specialists work to preserve the integrity of data while extracting information from sources such as computers, mobile devices, cloud environments, and Internet of Things (IoT) systems. The process involves strict adherence to legal and procedural standards to ensure that evidence is admissible in court. Its applications extend beyond criminal investigations to corporate security, incident response, and regulatory compliance.

DOI: 10.1201/9781003714811-3

Digital forensics faces unprecedented challenges in the age of AI-generated content. As synthetic media (particularly deepfakes) become increasingly realistic and widespread, traditional methods of verifying authenticity, tracing file origins, and managing evidence are being tested. Forensic experts must now adapt to detect and interpret deepfakes, analyse vast volumes of AI-generated data, and develop new tools and methodologies to preserve trust in digital evidence. A growing concern in this space is the phenomenon known as "AI slop," where AI detectors are trained on datasets that include AI-generated content, leading to unreliable or circular detection outcomes.

Deepfake forensics refers to the interdisciplinary field focused on detecting, analysing, and understanding synthetic media using digital forensic techniques. It draws on computer science, multimedia analysis, machine learning, and forensic principles to determine whether audio, video, or images have been artificially generated or manipulated. As the boundaries between real and synthetic content blur, deepfake forensics plays a critical role in safeguarding the integrity of digital communication, legal evidence, and public discourse.

Key challenges in this domain include:

Deepfakes and synthetic media quality: Highly realistic AI-generated videos and audio recordings have made it harder to rely on visual or auditory evidence. Forensic professionals now require advanced tools capable of detecting subtle anomalies or digital fingerprints left behind by deepfake creation tools and generative AI models. The rapid development and output quality of generation methods (e.g. diffusion models, transformer-based synthesis) continuously emerge, outpacing current detection capabilities.

Authenticity and attribution: Traditional digital forensic techniques (such as analysing metadata, file signatures, and known manipulation traces) are increasingly challenged by AI-generated content. These synthetic creations can closely replicate real-world data, making it difficult to distinguish between genuine and fabricated material using conventional methods. This growing sophistication undermines the reliability of traditional authenticity checks and demands more advanced detection strategies.

AI technologies also complicate attribution by obscuring the origin of digital content. Tracing material back to its original creator or source becomes significantly harder, posing major obstacles in investigations involving cybercrime, disinformation campaigns, and digital impersonation. The challenge is further amplified by the widespread sharing of deepfake media on social platforms, where compression processes degrade quality and strip away critical metadata, leaving investigators with limited forensic clues.

Scale and speed of generation: AI systems can produce vast quantities of content at unprecedented speeds, overwhelming traditional forensic workflows and increasing the difficulty of timely analysis and response. With lowered barriers to creation and minimal technical expertise required, the volume of synthetic content online continues to rise rapidly.

Detection tools also face notable limitations. Many models struggle to generalise beyond the specific types of deepfakes they were trained on, leading to reduced accuracy, inconsistent outputs, or complete failure when encountering new manipulation techniques. These issues are compounded by challenges within training datasets and model design, including dataset bias, limited representation of emerging deepfake methods, and the rapid evolution of generative technologies.

Lack of transparency and explainability: AI-based tools often lack the transparency required for courtroom use. Explainability refers to the ability of an AI system to make its decision-making process understandable and interpretable to humans. In digital forensics, this is especially critical when AI-generated conclusions are used as evidence in legal proceedings. This is explored further in Chapters 4 and 6. Also, the emergence of the "Liars Dividend" defence complicates the authentication of evidence being used in the court of law [1]. Defendants can claim that genuinely authentic media has been artificially generated and is a "deepfake," or is "fake news," creating a claim of uncertainty and doubt. Therefore, evidence authentication and integrity throughout the whole forensic process could be open to scrutiny.

While AI presents new challenges in digital forensics, it also offers valuable opportunities. From automating evidence triage to enhancing pattern recognition in large datasets, AI is increasingly being integrated into forensic workflows. It supports tasks such as anomaly detection, image and video authentication, and even predictive modelling for cybercrime investigations.

3.1.1 Transformative Benefits of AI in Forensic Investigations

Despite these challenges, AI and machine learning continue to offer substantial benefits for digital forensic analysis. They can rapidly process vast quantities of electronic evidence, streamlining tasks that once demanded extensive manual effort. AI-driven tools can automatically classify file types, extract metadata, and highlight potentially relevant material, thereby accelerating investigations and reducing the likelihood of human error. At the time of writing, OpenAI's most recent model release is GPT-5.2 [2], capable of advanced reasoning, long-context understanding, complex multi-step task execution, and high-performance knowledge work.

Key applications of AI in digital forensics include:

- *Automated evidence processing:* AI systems can rapidly ingest and organise vast datasets (such as disk images, cloud exports, mobile device extractions, email archives, and chat logs), sorting files by type, identifying duplicates, extracting metadata, and clustering similar content. This significantly reduces case timelines by allowing investigators to focus on the most relevant artefacts sooner, helping to reducing case timelines.
- *Code generation:* Tools like GPT-5 and its predecessors can assist in creating forensic code/scripts for data parsing, log analysis, and automation in live scenarios. Investigators can request code in Python, PowerShell, Bash, or other languages – useful in live response, triage automation, and rapid tooling development.
- *Knowledge retrieval:* LLMs can act as dynamic reference assistants, providing instant access to digital forensic standards

(e.g. ACPO, NIST, ISO), step-by-step procedural guidance, interpretation of artefacts, tool usage instructions, and explanations of platform-specific behaviours (e.g. Windows Registry, Android filesystem artefacts). This reduces dependency on static documentation and helps ensure procedural consistency during examinations.

- *Multilingual and cross-platform support:* LLMs interpret and translate forensic artefacts (including chat logs, social media posts, system messages, and embedded metadata) across dozens of languages, enabling smooth collaboration in international investigations. Helping analysts work confidently across heterogeneous environments.
- *Anomaly detection:* AI models trained on network behaviour, authentication logs, system events, and endpoint activity can highlight deviations from typical behaviour, such as unusual login patterns, unexpected data exfiltration routes, privilege escalation, or tampering with system artefacts. This helps surface indicators of compromise quickly and can reveal subtle manipulation attempts that would be easy to miss through manual review. Behaviour profiling models can also support insider threat investigations by flagging activity inconsistent with a user's normal patterns.
- *Training and education:* AI systems can generate realistic training scenarios, quizzes, simulated cases, and practice datasets tailored to specific learning objectives (e.g. cloud forensics or memory forensics). They can also create marking guides, assessment materials, and interactive walk-throughs, making forensic education more adaptive, engaging, and scalable.

AI also excels in multimedia and language analysis, enabling automated searches across images, videos, audio, and text. Applications include facial and object categorisation, character recognition, targeted image collection, language translation, and audio forensics such as speaker recognition and speech enhancement.

Recent studies highlight both the promise and limitations of AI in forensic contexts:

For example, Scanlon et al. evaluated ChatGPT (GPT-3.5 and GPT-4) across six forensic use cases, including artefact understanding, evidence searching, and anomaly detection.

While ChatGPT supported script generation and concept explanation, limitations included outdated data and hallucinations, making it unsuitable for high-risk tasks without oversight [3].

Michelet and Breitinger investigated the potential of using LLMs like ChatGPT-3.5 and LLaMA-2-13B to assist in digital forensic report generation. ChatGPT outperformed the locally run LLaMA-2-13B model in generating more accurate and complete texts. However, both models required significant human proofreading. Further, they found that while LLMs cannot fully automate report writing, they can still help with text summarisation and automating certain sections like "Introduction" [4].

Sharma et al.'s study concluded that *ForensicLLM*, a locally deployed LLaMA-3.1–8B model fine-tuned on forensic literature and curated artefacts, has demonstrated strong performance in source attribution and relevance, outperforming both base and retrieval-augmented models. However, there were questions regarding paper licensing and intellectual property [5].

However, the integration of AI into forensic workflows is not without risk. Practitioners must follow the evidence and corroborate data sources rather than relying uncritically on the output of automated systems. Identifying data as recorded is one aspect; understanding what that data actually means within its broader investigative context is another. Accepting an LLM's interpretation without scrutiny (especially when that interpretation cannot be fully explained, validated, or contextualised) risks severing the link between evidence and reasoning. Where speed and efficiency are prioritised over rigour, LLM use in digital forensics investigations can blur the boundary between discovery and interpretation, encouraging conclusions that are not grounded in the scientific method. True forensic practice requires triangulation, contextual assessment, and the examiner's professional judgement – none of which can be replaced by simply trusting an algorithmic response.

3.1.2 AI for Multimedia and Language Analysis

AI excels in automated searches across images, videos, audio, and text, enabling investigators to identify relevant evidence efficiently. Applications include:

- *Images and videos:* Facial and object categorisation, character recognition, targeted image collection, and elimination of irrelevant content.
- *Language:* Translation, pattern detection, and analysis of textual data such as emails, chats, and documents.
- *Audio forensics:* Automated speaker recognition, speech enhancement for clarity, anomaly detection in audio patterns, and real-time speaker authentication.

These capabilities are increasingly critical in a synthetic future where deepfake generation techniques evolve rapidly. AI systems can be trained on known manipulation patterns and continuously updated to recognise emerging threats, while predictive models anticipate new forms of digital deception before they become widespread.

AI's capacity to process and classify digital evidence has transformed how law enforcement addresses CSAM cases. These investigations often require reviewing vast quantities of distressing material, a task that is both time-consuming and psychologically demanding for investigators. Significant progress has been made in AI-powered categorisation and victim-identification tools, which help reduce this burden. For example, Semantics 21's *S21 VisionX* platform recently introduced AI Describe, the world's first secure, fully offline AI-based describer for CSAM and indecent material [6]. Operating entirely offline, it automatically generates detailed and consistent descriptions of images and videos while maintaining full forensic integrity, ultimately saving time and protecting investigator well-being. Similarly, tools such as Cellebrite Pathfinder automate the detection and classification of imagery, enabling faster, more efficient investigations and further alleviating the workload placed on those handling sensitive evidence.

A further tool of interest is *BelkaGPT*, the first fully offline AI assistant designed for digital forensic incident response (DFIR) investigations. It elevates investigative workflows by providing secure, efficient, and verifiable AI-driven insights while ensuring all data is processed locally to meet strict evidence-security requirements. It can automatically interpret and summarise a wide range of artefacts (including text communications, metadata, and media) and offers capabilities such as speech-to-text conversion, image content description, and picture categorisation to accelerate evidence discovery [7].

3.1.3 Other AI Uses in Law Enforcement

COMPAS (Correctional Offender Management Profiling for Alternative Sanctions) is an AI-based risk assessment tool widely used in US courts to predict the likelihood of a defendant reoffending. It analyses factors such as criminal history, age, and socio-economic background to generate a risk score that influences decisions on bail, sentencing, and parole. While COMPAS aims to provide objective, data-driven insights, it has faced criticism for lack of transparency and potential bias, particularly racial bias, because its proprietary algorithm is not publicly disclosed. Studies have shown that COMPAS can misclassify risk levels, raising ethical concerns about fairness and accountability in judicial processes. Its use highlights the growing tension between efficiency and equity in applying AI within the criminal justice system [8].

In England and Wales, similar concerns have emerged around the Offender Assessment System (OASys), the primary risk-assessment tool used by the Prison and Probation Service to evaluate offenders' risk and needs. OASys has been criticised for operating as a "black box" due to the lack of external access to the underlying data and for relying on criminal justice datasets already shown to be skewed against ethnic minorities, raising issues of transparency and potential structural bias. There are concerns about data accuracy, the reinforcement of historical bias, and the implications of automated decision-making in sentencing and parole [9].

AI has also proven invaluable in dismantling transnational criminal organisations (TNCOs). For example, a federal South American police force employed AI-powered investigative tools to disrupt the operations of an international drug cartel. Instead of concentrating on intercepting drug shipments (a tactic that often results only in the arrest of lower-level couriers) they used AI to trace financial networks, uncover money laundering pathways, and identify high-value assets connected to cartel leaders. This strategic use of AI enabled authorities to target the organisation's command structure directly, seizing assets linked to the kingpins and significantly weakening the cartel's operational capacity [10].

3.1.4 Traditional Media Forensics Versus Deepfake Forensics

Traditional file analysis is a core technique within digital forensics, involving the granular examination of files to identify their properties and uncover hidden, altered, or deleted information. This process typically includes analysing file headers, metadata, and structures to identify anomalies or reconstruct original content. Investigators use tools to inspect binary data, recover fragments from unallocated disk space, and verify file integrity through hash values. As such, traditional file analysis plays a crucial role in detecting tampering, validating authenticity, and tracing user activity, making it a foundational skill for forensic practitioners handling digital evidence.

While the core stages of digital forensics (evidence collection, analysis, and presentation) remain consistent, the emphasis placed on each stage can vary depending on the context. Certain scenarios may demand greater focus on specific phases or require tailored approaches to address unique challenges. There is a growing need for standardisation and transparency in digital forensic research methodologies. This would enable robust peer review, facilitate secondary analysis, and ensure the reliability and reproducibility of findings presented as contributions to knowledge [11].

However, relying solely on a general process model is insufficient to address the diverse nature of cybercrime and the wide array of cases encountered by law enforcement. To advance the field, it is essential to develop and adopt standardised case data formats, higher-level data abstractions, and practical models for forensic processing that can be consistently implemented across investigations.

In the UK, best practices for the seizure of digital evidence are outlined in the ACPO Good Practice Guide for Digital Evidence (v5.0) [12]. This guide provides detailed procedures for what can be seized, how it should be handled and transported, and the duration for which it may be retained. It also clarifies what types of information may be requested during a digital evidence search. These procedures are shaped by key UK legislation, including the Police and Criminal Evidence Act (PACE) 1984, the Regulation of Investigatory Powers

Act (RIPA) 2000, and the Criminal Justice and Police Act 2001. These laws govern the authority to access digital information and the legal grounds for seizing devices or data relevant to an investigation [13].

Despite the growing prevalence of AI-generated media, particularly deepfakes, there is currently no comprehensive or standardised guidance on how to handle such content within digital forensic investigations. The absence of clear protocols for identifying, preserving, and presenting deepfake evidence poses significant challenges for law enforcement and legal proceedings. As synthetic media becomes more sophisticated, the need for dedicated forensic methodologies and legal frameworks to address its implications is becoming increasingly urgent.

Detection techniques currently involve aspects of analysing:

- *Visual artefacts*: Identifying inconsistencies in lighting, shadows, facial movements, or blinking patterns.
- *Audio analysis*: Detecting unnatural speech patterns, mismatched lip-syncing, or synthetic voice signatures.
- *Model fingerprinting*: Tracing unique patterns left by specific AI models used to generate the content.

Multimedia forensic techniques enable investigators to answer critical questions about source identification and integrity verification, helping determine where a piece of digital content originated and whether it has been altered. As deepfakes and other forms of fabricated media become more sophisticated, analysts must devote significantly more time to examining them, since they are harder to detect and require detailed scrutiny. Differences in expertise and variation in the performance of analysis tools can also lead to conflicting interpretations. To meet these challenges, the forensic process must continue to evolve to incorporate robust authentication methods, enhanced processing, and granular examination of audio, video, and image content.

3.2 Deepfake Detection: Techniques and Indicators

Deepfake detection and the field of deepfake forensics relies on a combination of automated tools and expert human analysis to detect and interpret manipulated media. While AI and machine learning-powered detection systems play a crucial role in identifying synthetic content, manual visual inspection remains indispensable, particularly in high-stakes investigations where the authenticity of visual evidence must be verified with precision. Trained forensic analysts often examine content frame-by-frame to spot subtle anomalies such as unnatural facial expressions, inconsistent lighting, or mismatched reflections that automated systems may miss. The indispensable role of human oversight in interpreting and contextualising AI-generated insights is essential for maintaining accuracy and trust in digital forensic outcomes [10].

Several key manipulation techniques are commonly encountered in deepfake analysis [11]:

- *Face swapping:* In this approach, the face of one individual in a photo or video is replaced with another's, making it appear as though the second person was present or involved in the scene.
- *Face synthesis:* This technique generates entirely artificial faces using AI. These synthetic identities are often used in deepfake images and have been exploited for malicious purposes such as identity theft or document fraud.
- *Head puppetry:* This technique involves using a video of a person making head movements or facial expressions, then overlaying a synthetic version of another individual's face onto it. The result is a convincing illusion that the target person is performing those same movements or expressions.
- *Lip syncing and expression swapping:* This method manipulates an existing video of a person by altering their lip movements and facial expressions. Often combined with synthetic audio, it creates the impression that the subject is saying specific words or displaying emotions like happiness or anger.

Audio-based deepfakes introduce a distinct set of forensic challenges that extend beyond visual manipulation. Broadly, these techniques fall into three main categories, each presenting different risks and detection difficulties. *Imitation-based* methods modify existing audio recordings so that the speech appears to come from a different individual. By altering vocal characteristics such as pitch, tone, and timbre, these systems can convincingly mimic a target speaker's voice while retaining the original linguistic content.

Synthetic-based methods, on the other hand, generate speech entirely from text using advanced text-to-speech models. These systems produce fluent, natural-sounding audio that resembles human speech, and when paired with speaker embeddings or reference samples, they can closely approximate a specific person's voice. Finally, *replay-based* methods rely on capturing real audio from the target and reusing segments in combination with injected synthetic elements. By stitching together authentic and fabricated speech, these approaches create hybrid deepfakes that can be particularly difficult to detect because they blend genuine vocal features with manipulated content.

In addition to understanding manipulation techniques, forensic analysts rely on a range of visual and technical indicators to detect deepfakes. These cues often reveal subtle inconsistencies that distinguish synthetic media from authentic recordings.

- *Unnatural backgrounds:* Deepfake content may feature backgrounds that appear inconsistent with the original setting or contain visual anomalies. Techniques like double encoding analysis can reveal multiple rounds of compression, which is often a sign of tampering.
- *Inconsistent facial expressions:* Subtle irregularities in facial expressions (such as unnatural blinking, asymmetrical smiles, or delayed reactions) are common indicators in deepfake videos, revealing discrepancies between the synthetic overlay and natural human behaviour.
- *Unnatural movements:* Body movements in deepfake videos may appear stiff, disjointed, or out of sync with the rest of the body or environment, signalling that the content may have been artificially manipulated.
- *Audio inconsistencies:* Audio tracks in deepfake videos often fail to match lip movements or exhibit irregularities in tone, pitch, or sound quality. Misalignment between speech and visual cues is a common giveaway, particularly in low quality or hastily produced deepfakes.
- *Lighting, shadows, and reflections:* Inconsistencies in environmental lighting, shadow placement, or reflections often betray synthetic content. For example, facial highlights may not match the direction of ambient light, or reflections in glasses and mirrors may appear distorted or absent.

In some cases, deepfake detection tools may incorrectly classify manipulated media as "real" when the underlying image originates from a stock photo or another pre-existing source. Because the media is built on genuine visual material, automated systems may fail to flag the manipulation. In such situations, a reverse image search can be an effective forensic step, helping to reveal whether the content has been repurposed, altered, or lifted directly from an existing reference image.

Traditional detection methods also face limitations because they typically analyse audio or video in isolation. As deepfakes become increasingly multimodal (combining sophisticated visual manipulation with convincingly generated speech), approaches that focus on a single modality struggle to keep up. This growing complexity highlights the need for multimodal analysis, where audio-visual cues are evaluated together to provide a more reliable and comprehensive basis for forensic assessment [14].

3.3 Forensic Tools for Deepfake Detection and Analysis

Deepfake forensics involves identifying and analysing synthetic media generated using AI techniques. The tools used span across detection, authentication, and content analysis. A range of forensic tools has emerged to support the detection and analysis of deepfakes, each offering distinct capabilities for verifying the authenticity of digital media.

Amped Authenticate is a widely used forensic tool for image integrity analysis, employing techniques such as metadata inspection, noise pattern evaluation, and compression-artefact detection to identify signs of manipulation and assess whether an image has been altered. By revealing details about an image's origin and editing history, it helps investigators verify authenticity and maintain evidential integrity.

Complementing this, *Amped FIVE* focuses on enhancing and clarifying visual evidence. Designed for images and videos from sources such as CCTV, body-worn cameras, and mobile devices, it addresses issues like blur, poor lighting, perspective distortion, and unstable footage. Its comprehensive enhancement capabilities allow investigators to improve clarity while preserving forensic soundness, making it indispensable when working with degraded or complex media.

Microsoft Video Authenticator, developed to combat misinformation, evaluates facial blending and fading artefacts in videos to assign a confidence score indicating potential deepfake content.

Research-driven initiatives like *DARPA's MediFor and SemaFOR* programmes integrate semantic integrity checks, provenance analysis, and adversarial robustness to advance media forensics capabilities. *Reality Defender* provides real-time detection across platforms via browser extensions and APIs, supporting journalists and researchers in identifying synthetic media. *Sensity AI* offers enterprise-level monitoring of deepfake threats across social media, messaging apps, and the dark web, aiding governments and corporations in threat intelligence and brand protection. Finally, *Amber Video* uses blockchain technology to verify video provenance and detect tampering, ensuring trust in citizen journalism, legal evidence, and media reporting. Together, these tools form a critical part of the forensic response to synthetic media, supporting both investigative and preventative efforts in digital misinformation.

Table 3.1 highlights these forensic tools.

Table 3.1 Forensic Tools for Deepfake Detection and Analysis

TOOL	KEY FEATURES	PRIMARY USE CASE	FORENSIC TECHNIQUES
Amped Authenticate	- Metadata extraction - Error Level Analysis (ELA) - Clone detection - Camera model verification	Image and video authentication for law enforcement	Metadata analysis, Photo-Response Non-Uniformity (PRNU), ELA, clone detection
Amped FIVE	- Video/image enhancement - Deblurring and noise reduction - Perspective correction - Frame analysis	Processing, enhancing, and analysing video and image evidence for forensic investigation and court presentation	Image/video enhancement, stabilisation, colour correction, super-resolution, frame analysis
Microsoft Video Authenticator	- Frame-by-frame video analysis - Confidence scoring - Real-time detection	Deepfake detection, media authenticity verification, election integrity	AI-based anomaly detection, pixel-level analysis
DARPA MediFor/SemaFOR	- Semantic analysis - Provenance tracking - Multimodal detection	Media integrity assessment, manipulation detection, and provenance analysis for defence and intelligence applications	Content provenance, semantic consistency checks

TOOL	KEY FEATURES	PRIMARY USE CASE	FORENSIC TECHNIQUES
Reality Defender	- Multimodal detection (image, video, audio, text) - Explainable AI reports - Real-time monitoring	Enterprise security, media verification, fraud prevention	AI-based detection, anomaly scoring, cross-modal analysis
Sensity AI	- Visual fingerprinting - API integration - Large-scale monitoring	Enterprise security, identity verification, law enforcement, and threat intelligence	Image/video fingerprinting, metadata correlation
Amber Video	- Blockchain-based provenance - Tamper-proof timestamping - Capture authentication	Authentication of video evidence in legal proceedings	Blockchain ledger, cryptographic signatures

Alongside automated detection tools, forensic techniques such as reference image comparison, social media source identification, clone detection, and in-depth analysis beyond simple "AI or not" classification are essential for ensuring accuracy and reliability. Specifically:

- *Reference image comparison:* Many detection systems use reference images from trusted sources (such as Flickr or verified archives) to compare against suspect files. This process involves analysing image properties, including metadata, camera make and model, and encoding signatures, to identify inconsistencies. File analysis comparison can reveal whether the suspect media aligns with known authentic samples or exhibits anomalies indicative of manipulation.
- *Social media identification:* Some tools include a social media identification feature, which detects whether an image's properties suggest it was sourced from a platform like Instagram or TikTok. This is important because platform-level compression and metadata stripping often obscure forensic markers, complicating authenticity checks.
- *Clone detection:* Advanced systems incorporate clone detection, which identifies duplicated or altered regions within an image. This technique can reveal whether objects have been added, removed, or copied from other sources, which is a common tactic in synthetic media creation.
- *Beyond "AI or not":* A simple binary approach (classifying content as AI-generated or not) is insufficient. While such

classifiers can flag synthetic origins, they do not account for other manipulations that may occur in authentic media. Forensic analysis must go deeper, examining shadow consistency, reflection patterns, and geometric alignment [11]. Moreover, different forensic tools often produce varying results, underscoring the need for multi-tool validation and expert interpretation to ensure accuracy and reliability.

3.4 Procedural Challenges in Forensic Practice

The rise of deepfake technology has introduced complex obstacles for forensic practitioners, reshaping how evidence is collected, analysed, and validated. Advances in manipulation techniques have eroded traditional forensic markers, making detection increasingly difficult across multiple formats such as video, audio, and images. These technical and procedural challenges are compounded by platform-level compression, which strips critical metadata and visual cues, and by the absence of standardised protocols for handling AI-generated evidence. Together, these factors create significant procedural and legal uncertainties, demanding new frameworks and adaptive strategies to maintain forensic integrity:

- *Widespread accessibility:* Deepfake technology has moved from the domain of skilled professionals to the general public. Rapid advancements in AI and the proliferation of social media platforms mean that even non-experts can now create highly convincing synthetic media. These creations can be distributed at scale and with unprecedented speed, amplifying the risk of misinformation, fraud, and reputational harm.
- *Sophisticated manipulation:* Modern deepfake tools are increasingly capable of removing or obscuring forensic artefacts that traditionally signalled manipulation. This makes detection significantly harder, as reliable indicators are often absent or degraded [14–16]. The challenge is compounded by the diversity of formats (i.e. video, audio, images, and text), each requiring distinct detection strategies. Developing systems that can handle this range without becoming overly specialised remains a complex task.
- *Data and platform compression:* Compression techniques, whether applied during file creation or by social media

platforms, degrade subtle visual and audio cues essential for forensic analysis. When media is uploaded, platform-level compression often strips away critical metadata and forensic markers, making it difficult to trace origin or verify authenticity. This loss of detail severely limits the effectiveness of detection tools.

- *Lack of standardised protocols:* Currently, there is no universally accepted framework for collecting, analysing, and presenting deepfake evidence. This absence of standardisation complicates validation and comparison across jurisdictions and institutions. Legal uncertainty further exacerbates the issue, as courts lack clear guidelines on the admissibility and reliability of AI-generated evidence, raising concerns about fairness, transparency, and due process.

3.4.1 Data Integrity and Cross-Platform Variability

Deepfake detection systems often rely on limited datasets, typically focused on a single modality such as video or audio. This narrow scope reduces robustness in real-world scenarios where deepfakes vary widely in format, quality, and manipulation techniques. For example, a detector trained exclusively on high-resolution video may fail when confronted with compressed social media clips or low quality live streams. Similarly, audio-based systems often struggle with multilingual content or recordings degraded by background noise.

A further complicating factor is cross-platform variability. Each platform (whether Facebook, TikTok, YouTube, or messaging apps) applies its own compression algorithms, metadata handling, and file transformation processes. These operations frequently strip away or alter critical forensic markers such as pixel-level inconsistencies, encoding signatures, and embedded metadata. As a result, forensic tools that rely on these markers for authenticity checks may produce false negatives or fail entirely when analysing content that has passed through multiple platforms.

In addition, compression and transcoding can introduce artefacts that mimic deepfake indicators, further confusing detection systems. This variability not only affects detection accuracy but also complicates chain-of-custody verification, as the original file's integrity is compromised during distribution. Without standardised protocols for preserving forensic markers across platforms, investigators face significant challenges in tracing content origins and validating authenticity.

3.4.2 Underexplored Audiovisual Dimensions

Many detection systems fail to account for cultural nuances, emotional cues, and language-specific features that influence authenticity. Real-time detection remains underdeveloped, despite its importance for social media and live broadcasts where deepfakes can spread rapidly. Similarly, emotional cues (such as tone, tempo, and micro-expressions) are often overlooked, reducing the accuracy of systems designed to identify manipulations in sensitive contexts like political speeches or personal communications.

There is ongoing research exploring solutions to the critical gap in real-time deepfake detection. While most forensic tools are designed for post-distribution analysis, they are rarely optimised for live environments such as social media streams, video conferencing, or broadcast media. This limitation is significant because deepfakes can spread virally within minutes, influencing public opinion or causing reputational harm before detection occurs. Real-time detection requires lightweight, high-speed algorithms capable of operating at scale without compromising accuracy; a challenge that remains difficult to solve.

Recent work, such as the Locally Aware Deepfake Detection Algorithm (LaDeDa) and its efficient variant Tiny-LaDeDa, demonstrates progress towards real-time solutions [17]. These models use patch-based analysis to detect subtle generation artefacts and achieve high accuracy while being computationally efficient enough for edge devices. Despite promising results (such as 93.7% accuracy on real-world datasets), researchers note that reliable real-time detection for social media and live broadcasts is still an unsolved problem, highlighting the need for further innovation in this area.

3.4.3 Proactive Measures Remain Limited

Preventative strategies such as digital watermarking and adversarial defences remain in their infancy and are not yet widely integrated into forensic workflows. Digital watermarking involves embedding imperceptible markers within media files to verify authenticity and trace origin, but adoption is limited due to interoperability issues and lack of standardisation across platforms. Similarly, adversarial defences (techniques designed to make AI-generated content detectable or resistant to manipulation) are still experimental and often fail under real-world conditions where attackers can adapt quickly.

The absence of these proactive measures means that forensic efforts are largely reactive, focusing on detection after harm has occurred rather than prevention. Without robust, universally accepted watermarking protocols and resilient adversarial strategies, the ability to trace or block manipulations before they spread remains severely constrained, leaving individuals and institutions vulnerable to reputational, financial, and security risks.

3.5 Emerging Preventative Technologies

While current forensic approaches are largely reactive, several proactive strategies are being developed to prevent or trace deepfake manipulations before they cause harm. These technologies aim to embed authenticity markers at the point of content creation and ensure traceability across platforms. Below are some examples of emerging preventative technologies:

- *Digital watermarking:*
  This involves embedding imperceptible markers within media files to verify authenticity and trace origin. These markers can be cryptographic or algorithmic, allowing forensic tools to confirm whether content has been altered. However, widespread adoption is hindered by interoperability issues, lack of standardisation, and resistance from platforms concerned about performance and user experience.
- *Platform-level traceability:*
  Social media and content-sharing platforms are increasingly exploring traceability features, such as metadata preservation and AI-driven authenticity checks. These measures aim to maintain forensic markers during compression and distribution, reducing the risk of losing critical data needed for detection.

- *Adversarial defences:*
  Adversarial defences involve designing content or detection systems that resist manipulation or make synthetic alterations easier to identify. Techniques include embedding perturbations that disrupt deepfake generation or training detection models to recognise adversarial patterns. While promising, these methods are still experimental and require further research to ensure robustness against adaptive attackers.
- *Cryptographic signatures:*
  Cryptographic signing of media files ensures that any alteration invalidates the signature, providing a strong mechanism for authenticity verification. Standards such as C2PA (Coalition for Content Provenance and Authenticity) are emerging to promote adoption across industries, enabling platforms and forensic tools to verify content integrity at scale. In addition to cryptographic signatures, users can embed watermarks or unique identifiers in their uploaded media. These measures serve two purposes: they can "poison" deepfake creation by introducing detectable markers and embed clear provenance signatures, helping investigators trace the origin and confirm authenticity even after distribution.

3.5.1 Blockchain-Based Provenance

Blockchain technology provides a decentralised, tamper-proof ledger for recording the origin and modification history of digital content. By registering media files on a blockchain, creators can establish immutable proof of authenticity, creating a transparent chain of custody that is resistant to alteration. This approach is gaining traction in sectors such as journalism, intellectual property protection, and digital rights management, where trust and verifiability are critical.

Blockchain-based provenance can help identify deepfakes and track manipulations in publicly shared media, including content involving government officials or other high-profile figures. By embedding unique identifiers or cryptographic hashes at the point of creation, investigators can verify whether a file has been altered at any stage. While scalability and integration with mainstream platforms remain challenges, the potential for blockchain to provide a universal standard for content authenticity makes it a promising solution for combating synthetic media and misinformation.

3.6 Summary

In the age of AI-generated content, digital forensics faces a rapidly evolving landscape where traditional methods of media authentication are increasingly challenged. While conventional media forensics focused on verifying the integrity of original files and identifying basic manipulations, deepfake forensics demands more advanced techniques to detect highly realistic synthetic media. This emerging field combines machine learning, multimedia analysis, and forensic expertise to identify manipulations in both audio and visual streams. A range of tools and techniques (such as head puppetry detection, lip-sync analysis, and multimodal anomaly detection) are now employed alongside manual frame-by-frame inspection to ensure accuracy. Nevertheless, the field faces significant technical and procedural challenges, including the unreliability of detectors and outputs (with some trained on synthetic data (AI slop)), the limitations of monomodal detection methods, and the need for scalable solutions that preserve evidentiary integrity. As deepfakes grow more sophisticated, the integration of human expertise with intelligent forensic systems becomes essential to maintaining trust in digital evidence.

References

[1] B. Chesney and D. Citron, 'Deep fakes: A looming challenge for privacy, democracy, and national security', *California Law Review*, vol. 107, no. 6, pp. 1753–1820, 2019, doi: 10.15779/Z38RV0D15J.

[2] OpenAI, 'GPT-5.2', *Open AI Platform*. Available: https://platform.openai.com/docs/models/gpt-5.2.

[3] M. Scanlon, F. Breitinger, C. Hargreaves, J. N. Hilgert, and J. Sheppard, 'ChatGPT for digital forensic investigation: The good, the bad, and the unknown', *Forensic Science International: Digital Investigation*, vol. 46, Oct. 2023, doi: 10.1016/j.fsidi.2023.301609.

[4] G. Michelet and F. Breitinger, 'ChatGPT, Llama, can you write my report? An experiment on assisted digital forensics reports written using (local) large language models', *Forensic Science International: Digital Investigation*, vol. 48, Mar. 2024, doi: 10.1016/j.fsidi.2023.301683.

[5] B. Sharma, J. Ghawaly, K. McCleary, A. M. Webb, and I. Baggili, 'ForensicLLM: A local large language model for digital forensics', *Forensic Science International: Digital Investigation*, vol. 52, Mar. 2025, doi: 10.1016/j.fsidi.2025.301872.

[6] Semantics 21, 'The world's most advanced AI platform for CSAM categorisation and victim identification', *Semantics 21*. Available: www.semantics21.com/s21-visionx/.

[7] Belkasoft, 'BelkaGPT—The first offline AI assistant for DFIR investigations', 2025. Available: https://belkasoft.com/belkagpt.

[8] M. Vaccaro and J. Waldo, 'Algorithms in human decision-making: A case study with the COMPAS risk assessment software', Bachelor's thesis, Harvard College. Mar. 2019. Available: https://dash.harvard.edu/server/api/core/bitstreams/fc1ba31b-3413-44e6-b066-85cb602cf7c2/content.

[9] L. Hamilton and P. Ugwudike, 'A "black box" AI system has been influencing criminal justice decisions for over two decades – It's time to open it up', *The Conversation*. Available: https://theconversation.com/a-black-box-ai-system-has-been-influencing-criminal-justice-decisions-for-over-two-decades-its-time-to-open-it-up-200594.

[10] Police1, 'Policing with a digital partner: Preparing law enforcement for the age of AI', Available: https://www.police1.com/leadership-institute/policing-with-a-digital-partner-preparing-law-enforcement-for-the-age-of-ai

[11] Á. MacDermott, 'Deepfake forensics: Exploring the impact and implications of fabricated media in digital forensic investigations – DFRWS EU poster', in *Digital Forensics Research Workshop Europe (DFRWS EU 2025). Brno, Czech Republic*, 2025. Accessed: Apr. 3, 2025. Available: https://dfrws.org/wp-content/uploads/2025/04/DFRWS_EU_2025_paperposter_115.pdf.

[12] ACPO (Association of Chief Police Officers), 'ACPO Good Practice Guide for Digital Evidence', London, Oct. 2011. Available: https://npcc.police.uk/documents/crime/2014/Revised%20Good%20Practice%20Guide%20for%20Digital%20Evidence_Vers%205_Oct%202011_Website.pdf.

[13] P. Office of Science, 'Digital Forensics and Crime', London, Mar. 2016. Available: www.parliament.uk/post

[14] I. Amerini *et al.*, 'Deepfake media forensics: State of the art and challenges ahead', Aug. 2024. Available: http://arxiv.org/abs/2408.00388

[15] I. Amerini *et al.*, 'Deepfake media forensics: Status and future challenges', *Journal of Imaging*, vol. 11, no. 3, Mar. 2025, doi: 10.3390/jimaging11030073.

[16] G. Bendiab, H. Haiouni, I. Moulas, and S. Shiaeles, 'Deepfakes in digital media forensics: Generation, AI-based detection and challenges', *Journal of Information Security and Applications*, vol. 88, Feb. 2025, doi: 10.1016/j.jisa.2024.103935.

[17] B. Cavia, E. Horwitz, T. Reiss, and Y. Hoshen, 'Real-time deepfake detection in the real-world', Jun. 2024. Available: http://arxiv.org/abs/2406.09398

4

Case Studies

Deepfakes in Criminal Investigations

As deepfake technologies become more accessible and convincing, their presence in criminal investigations is no longer hypothetical. It is a growing reality with tangible consequences. This chapter examines real-world incidents where manipulated media has complicated investigative processes, delayed justice, or misled law enforcement. Through a series of case studies, we explore the criminal uses of deepfakes in fraud, extortion, and harassment; the challenges they pose when introduced as evidence in forensic workflows and courtroom proceedings, and high-profile examples that illustrate the broader societal and legal implications of synthetic media. These cases offer critical insights into how digital forensics must adapt to detect, interpret, and respond to deepfakes in the pursuit of truth and accountability.

4.1 Criminal Uses of Deepfakes: Fraud, Extortion, and Harassment

The rapid proliferation of AI is reshaping criminal markets, creating new opportunities for illicit activities while introducing operational challenges for offenders. Deepfakes have become a powerful tool for crimes such as financial fraud, extortion, harassment, and the production of synthetic NCII and CSAM. These areas are particularly lucrative, attracting both organised criminal networks and opportunistic threat actors. The accessibility of generative AI tools lowers technical barriers, enabling large-scale manipulation and making sophisticated attacks easier to execute.

Despite this growth, criminal groups face adoption bottlenecks that law enforcement can exploit. Challenges include the need for advanced technical expertise, access to high-performance computing resources, robust operational security, and the reliability of AI systems themselves

 DOI: 10.1201/9781003714811-4

[1]. Additionally, offenders increasingly use AI to create fake avatars, fabricate online profiles, and generate persuasive scripts for scams – further blurring the line between authentic and synthetic identities. These tactics amplify social engineering attacks, which exploit human psychology rather than technical vulnerabilities to deceive individuals into revealing sensitive information or performing compromising actions. Common methods include phishing, impersonation, and pretexting, all of which become more convincing when powered by realistic deepfake content. This convergence of AI and social engineering makes detection and prevention significantly more complex.

4.1.1 Deepfakes as a Tool for Fraud and Strategic Deception

Deepfakes are increasingly deployed to deceive institutions and individuals for financial or strategic gain. Criminals exploit hyper-realistic synthetic media to impersonate executives during video calls, authorising fraudulent transactions or influencing high stakes negotiations. These attacks leverage trust in visual and auditory cues, making traditional security measures vulnerable and amplifying the risk of large-scale financial fraud. For example:

- **Executive impersonation:** In 2023, a Hong Kong finance worker was tricked into transferring $25 million USD after a video call with a deepfake CEO – a case illustrating the growing sophistication of business email compromise attacks [2].
- **Document forgery:** AI-generated passports and ID cards have been used to bypass onboarding checks in cryptocurrency exchanges – undermining Know Your Customer (KYC) protocols [3].
- **Synthetic biometrics:** Fraudsters employ deepfake avatars to defeat facial recognition systems in banking and e-government services [4].
- **Fake job interviews:** In 2024, US tech firms reported incidents where AI-generated candidates passed remote interviews to gain access to sensitive systems.
- **Market manipulation:** Fabricated videos of CEOs making false announcements have triggered short term volatility in stock prices.

- **Tampering with digital evidence:** Altered CCTV footage and fabricated confessions have been documented in organised crime investigations, complicating evidential integrity.

These tactics highlight how generative AI lowers technical barriers for criminals, enabling scalable and convincing fraud schemes that exploit human trust and institutional processes.

4.1.2 Extortion and Coercion

Deepfakes are increasingly weaponised as tools of coercion, often used to exert financial or reputational pressure on victims. One of the most prevalent forms is non-consensual pornography, where a victim's face is superimposed onto explicit content to intimidate or extort payments. Equally concerning is the rise of synthetic CSAM, with law enforcement agencies reporting a surge in AI-generated content used for exploitation and intimidation [5]. Criminals also fabricate compromising media to create fabricated threats, pressuring individuals or institutions into compliance.

Beyond these tactics, romance scams have escalated dramatically, with AI-generated personas building trust before exploiting victims financially, a trend highlighted in recent threat assessments. Increasingly, youths are being targeted in these schemes through social media platforms, where perpetrators exploit trust and vulnerability to initiate coercive interactions. This growing trend underscores the urgent need for education, awareness, and stronger safeguards to protect younger users from manipulation and exploitation online. In response, the UK announced in November 2025 that lessons on deepfakes and synthetic media will be introduced into school curriculums as part of a major digital literacy initiative, scheduled for implementation in September 2028, aiming to equip students with critical thinking skills and resilience against online manipulation [6].

4.1.3 Harassment and Psychological Harm

Deepfakes have also emerged as a tool for targeted harassment, used to shame, silence, or cause psychological harm to individuals. These attacks exploit the perceived authenticity of synthetic media, making victims vulnerable to reputational damage and emotional distress. These include:

- **Online humiliation:** AI-generated content is increasingly used to produce defamatory or embarrassing material aimed at activists, journalists, and private individuals.
- **Non-consensual pornography/NCII:** Victims' faces are superimposed onto explicit content without consent, often shared widely to cause emotional harm and reputational damage.
- **Synthetic CSAM:** Deepfake technology can generate synthetic CSAM, posing severe challenges for law enforcement and victim identification. In some cases, these synthetic images or videos may be derived from real materials, further complicating detection and raising ethical and legal concerns.
- **Political and social manipulation:** Deepfakes are deployed to spread disinformation, polarise communities, and incite unrest. For example, a deepfake video of Ukrainian President Volodymyr Zelenskyy urging soldiers to surrender circulated widely during the Russia-Ukraine conflict, undermining trust and fuelling confusion.
- **Extremist propaganda:** Synthetic media enables the creation of fabricated speeches or videos endorsing radical ideologies, serving as recruitment tools for extremist groups. These manipulations exploit emotional triggers and perceived authenticity to radicalise vulnerable individuals.

The psychological impact of deepfake harassment is profound, with victims often experiencing severe stress, anxiety, and reputational harm. This is compounded by the credibility effect: the tendency for viewers to trust visual evidence even when fabricated. Research shows that exposure to deepfakes erodes public trust, amplifies disinformation, and inflicts lasting emotional damage [7, 8].

In educational settings, deepfake cyberbullying has emerged as a serious threat. Students have been targeted with synthetic videos depicting compromising scenarios, leading to social ostracism and long-term psychological scars. Laczi and Poser emphasise the heightened risks for vulnerable age groups, including children, who are particularly susceptible to emotional harm and reputational damage [9].

While deepfake technology offers potential benefits, its predominant use remains harmful. The increasing sophistication of these techniques makes detecting false content progressively more challenging, enabling manipulation, deception, and the creation of emotionally damaging material at scale. This growing threat underscores the urgent need for robust detection tools, legal frameworks, and educational initiatives to mitigate harm and protect victims.

4.1.4 Disinformation and Political Manipulation

Deepfakes have become powerful tools for distributing disinformation and manipulating public opinion. They are increasingly deployed during elections, public health crises, and geopolitical conflicts to spread false narratives that erode trust in institutions and media. By presenting fabricated content as authentic, these manipulations can mislead voters, distort policy debates, and undermine democratic processes.

Extremist and terrorist groups also exploit deepfake technology to support their narratives. Fabricated speeches, staged martyrdom videos, and falsified depictions of enemy atrocities are used to recruit followers, incite violence, and amplify propaganda [10]. Such content not only fuels radicalisation but also complicates efforts by law enforcement and intelligence agencies to counter extremist messaging. Beyond targeted propaganda, deepfakes can stoke social unrest and deepen political polarisation. Manipulated media is often deployed to inflame tensions between communities, simulate hate speech, or misrepresent protest movements, creating conditions that may lead to real-world violence. These tactics exploit existing societal divisions, amplifying discord and mistrust.

As outlined in Chapter 1, social media platforms remain the primary channels for disseminating deepfake and fabricated media. The rapid spread of such content is facilitated by users who accept what they see and read online without questioning its authenticity. This tendency to take information at face value is further amplified by algorithms that prioritise engagement over accuracy, frequently promoting sensational or emotionally charged content regardless of its truthfulness. In this environment, manipulated media can gain traction quickly, shaping public perception and complicating efforts to verify facts or counter misinformation.

4.1.5 Global Legislative Responses to Deepfake and Non-Consensual Imagery

Legislation addressing the creation and distribution of deepfakes and non-consensual imagery is advancing globally, reflecting growing awareness of the harms posed by synthetic media. In the United Kingdom (UK), the Online Safety Act 2023 (enforced from January 2024) introduced criminal offences for sharing intimate deepfake content without consent. These offences were designated as "priority," requiring platforms to proactively detect and remove such material or face enforcement action by Ofcom. Building on this framework, the UK government announced in January 2025 new offences under the Crime and Policing Bill, including criminalising the creation of sexually explicit deepfakes, the non-consensual taking of intimate images, and the installation of equipment intended for such abuse [11]. However, as of January 2026, these measures are not fully implemented.

Ofcom has launched a formal investigation under the Online Safety Act into whether X complied with its legal duties to protect UK users from illegal content: specifically, non-consensual intimate images (NCII) and sexualised content generated via X's AI tool, Grok. Allegations include the generation and sharing of illegal intimate image abuse and CSAM, prompting global political support for stricter enforcement. Under the Act, platforms must: (1) take appropriate steps to prevent UK users from accessing illegal content, including non-consensual intimate images and CSAM; (2) conduct regular risk assessments when introducing significant features such as image-generating AI; and (3) swiftly remove illegal content when notified, supported by robust safeguarding systems. Failure to comply constitutes a breach of legal obligations.

Recent UK government action has accelerated efforts to make the creation or solicitation of NCII a criminal offence, integrating these provisions into priority Online Safety obligations. The creation and distribution of non-consensual deepfakes is already illegal under UK law, and platforms like X are expected to implement measures preventing such material from appearing in the UK. Initial responses from X and

Elon Musk have framed these requirements as an infringement on freedom of speech, and as of January 2026, discussions are underway about banning X in the UK, with reports of users leaving the platform amid growing controversy.

In the US, the Senate has unanimously passed the DEFIANCE Act of 2025, S.1837 (formerly the Disrupt Explicit Forged Images and Non-Consensual Edits Act), which was reintroduced and passed in the Senate again in January 2026. The bill continues through legislative processes towards full enactment. The DEFIANCE Act is legislation establishing a federal civil right of action for individuals harmed by non-consensual, sexually explicit AI-generated images. This allows victims to sue the creators of such content. The bill specifically addresses the recent surge in harmful material linked to Grok's image-generation technology. Building on the earlier "Take It Down Act" (signed into law in May 2025), the DEFIANCE Act marks the first federal law to criminalise the publication of non-consensual intimate imagery, including AI-generated deepfakes. It also requires online platforms to remove reported content within 48 hours, with enforcement overseen by the Federal Trade Commission.

Similarly, in the US, many users are leaving X. The American Federation of Teachers (AFT) representing 1.8 million educators, announced it is leaving X, citing harmful AI-generated images of minors and adults as a breaking point. This move reflects a broader public backlash in the US against platforms that allow non-consensual imagery to proliferate [12].

Denmark has taken a pioneering approach by passing a copyright law amendment in 2025 that grants individuals legal ownership over their likeness (including face, voice, and body). This empowers citizens to demand takedowns of AI-generated imitations and seek compensation for misuse. The law is expected to come into full effect by early 2026 and has drawn interest from other EU member states as a potential model for broader digital identity protections.

In the European Union (EU), the Artificial Intelligence (AI) Act (Regulation EU 2024/1689) was adopted in June 2024 and began phased enforcement in August 2025. It bans harmful uses of AI-based identity manipulation and requires clear labelling of AI-generated content. The Act introduces a risk-based framework for AI governance, with stricter obligations for high-risk systems and general-purpose AI models.

Together, these legislative efforts signal a growing international commitment to protecting individuals from digital impersonation, exploitation, and misinformation. While enforcement and cross-border coordination remain complex, the legal landscape is evolving to meet the challenges posed by synthetic media and AI-driven abuse.

4.2 Deepfakes as Evidence: Forensic Response and Courtroom Impact

There is a significant gap in training for judges and legal professionals on how to evaluate, rule on, and interact with deepfake and AI-generated media in judicial proceedings. Without clear guidance or specialised education, courts risk inconsistent rulings and compromised evidentiary standards when synthetic content is introduced as evidence.

A landmark case in Washington State (2024) illustrates this challenge: a judge prohibited the use of AI-enhanced CCTV footage in a triple murder trial, ruling that such evidence could mislead juries and introduce "information that was never there." The court emphasised that AI enhancement relies on opaque, non-peer-reviewed methods, making it unreliable for evidentiary purposes [13]. This decision underscores growing judicial concern over manipulated media and its potential to distort justice.

While AI offers significant opportunities to improve efficiency within the legal system, its complexity and lack of transparency often conflict with fundamental principles of fairness and accountability. Ensuring that evidence remains sound and legal processes remain open to scrutiny is becoming increasingly difficult in an era of synthetic media.

Neural network systems often rely on probabilistic processes, meaning that running the same image through an AI model twice can produce different outputs. This variability poses a serious challenge for forensic integrity, where consistency and reproducibility are essential. In traditional forensics, there is an absolute truth e.g. blood group tests cannot alter biological reality. By contrast, digital evidence is far more vulnerable to distortion. Even seemingly minor enhancements, such as adjusting contrast or brightness, may clarify details but can also alter the evidential narrative. More invasive edits fundamentally change what is visible, raising questions about authenticity.

As Dr Karl Jones (LJMU) aptly states, "it is no longer the truth; evidentially, it is corrupted." This principle is critical when explaining to law enforcement the implications of AI-enhanced media in court. For instance, if CCTV footage is processed through AI to "improve" clarity, every pixel and frame becomes a modified version of reality. While the underlying story (such as a person's actions) may remain intact, investigators must explicitly caution juries to focus only on those actions and disregard altered visual elements like colour or lighting. Failure to do so risks misrepresenting evidence and undermining judicial trust [14].

Detection confidence adds another layer of complexity. If investigators do not know what anomalies to look for, they may struggle to identify deepfakes. Subtle inconsistencies (such as unnatural lighting, mismatched reflections, or irregular facial movements) can easily be overlooked unless practitioners are trained to recognise them. This highlights the urgent need for specialised training and explainable AI tools to support forensic professionals in maintaining evidential integrity.

The growing trend of introducing fabricated media sourced from social platforms into judicial proceedings is significantly increasing the complexity of source verification and origin authentication. Courts are now confronted with the challenge of distinguishing genuine evidence from AI-generated or manipulated content, as social media often lacks robust provenance mechanisms. This issue is compounded by the ease with which synthetic media can be created and disseminated, eroding traditional assumptions about the reliability of visual and audio evidence.

Media manipulation in legal contexts is also gaining prominence online, with deepfakes being used not only for harassment and disinformation but also for evidentiary distortion. One emerging tactic involves the creation of fake alibis, where defendants attempt to fabricate proof of their presence at alternative locations during the time of an offence. Although documented cases remain limited, recent trends indicate a growing willingness to exploit deepfake technology for judicial deception. Examples include AI-generated videos depicting suspects at different venues, voice-cloned audio suggesting phone calls or conversations elsewhere and manipulated CCTV footage with altered timestamps or swapped faces. These practices pose severe risks to evidential integrity and highlight the urgent need for standardised forensic protocols and explainable AI tools to authenticate digital evidence.

4.3 High-Profile Cases of Media Manipulation

4.3.1 The Mendones Case: A Landmark Deepfake Evidence Ruling (2025)

The *Mendones v. Cushman & Wakefield, Inc.* case in California is one of the first major reported instances where a court directly confronted deepfake evidence [15]. On 9 September 2025, the Superior Court of California, Alameda County, dismissed the case with prejudice after determining that the self-represented plaintiffs had submitted fabricated evidence (including deepfake videos and altered images) in support of their motion for summary judgment.

The court found that several exhibits, including short looping video clips and manipulated photographs, were generated using generative AI. These videos featured robotic speech, unnatural lip movements, and inconsistent metadata, all of which raised red flags. Judge Victoria Kolakowski concluded that the plaintiffs violated California Code of Civil Procedure §128.7, which requires parties to certify that their submissions are truthful and not presented for improper purposes.

Rather than imposing monetary or evidentiary sanctions, the court applied the most severe remedy: terminating sanctions, striking the complaint and dismissing the case entirely. The ruling emphasised that deepfake evidence fundamentally undermines judicial integrity and sent a strong deterrent message – courts will maintain zero tolerance for AI-generated falsifications. Legal experts have described this case as a "warning shot," highlighting the urgent need for clear rules and technical safeguards as deepfakes enter the courtroom.

4.3.2 USA v. Khalilian (2024)

In July 2024, in *USA v. Khalilian,* Fereidoun "Fred" Khalilian pleaded guilty to witness tampering and was sentenced to two years in prison as part of a murder-for-hire and extortion scheme in Nevada. The case gained significant attention for his unsuccessful use of a "deepfake defence" to challenge voice recordings used as evidence [16, 17].

Khalilian was a Florida entrepreneur notorious for failed online poker ventures and elaborate scams. He created a false persona of royalty to strengthen his credibility and attract investors. In late 2023, Khalilian was indicted for a murder-for-hire plot and conspiracy to commit witness tampering. Prosecutors alleged that he hired a bodyguard to kill a filmmaker who was producing a documentary exposing his history of fraudulent dealings. Additionally, Khalilian reportedly left threatening voice messages for the filmmaker. Central to the case were audio recordings of these threatening messages, which prosecutors claimed were left by Khalilian.

The defence counsel argued that voice recordings could be deepfaked, challenging their admissibility. While the court ultimately accepted the evidence based on witness familiarity, the case illustrates how AI can be invoked to dispute or fabricate evidence [16]. In an unprecedented legal tactic, Khalilian's attorneys sought to exclude voice recordings by arguing they could be a deepfake. The defence claimed that the rapid advancement of generative AI made it impossible to verify the recordings' authenticity beyond mere speculation.

The judge dismissed the deepfake argument, noting that the prosecution could authenticate the recordings through testimony from individuals familiar with Khalilian's voice. The court remarked this would likely suffice, signalling that the deepfake claim did not pose a serious challenge to the evidence. Following this ruling, Khalilian accepted a plea deal, admitting guilt to one count of witness tampering. In July 2024, a federal judge in Nevada sentenced Khalilian to two years in prison.

The *USA v. Khalilian* case [16] serves as an important early indicator of how courts may approach deepfake-related evidence in criminal proceedings. Legal analysts note that the ruling underscores the limitations of relying on a speculative "deepfake defense" to challenge otherwise credible evidence. The outcome suggests that, at least for now, traditional authentication methods (such as witness familiarity) remain sufficient to admit evidence when allegations of manipulation lack concrete proof. This sets a precedent whereby courts will likely require demonstrable evidence of tampering before excluding media based on potential deepfake fabrication.

4.3.3 Wisconsin v. Rittenhouse: The Rittenhouse Trial and the Pinch-to-Zoom Dispute (2021)

In November 2021, in *Wisconsin v. Rittenhouse,* during Kyle Rittenhouse's trial, the defence successfully blocked the prosecution's attempt to zoom in on video evidence using an iPad's pinch-to-zoom feature. The defence argued that Apple's software might employ AI to generate additional pixels, potentially altering the original footage. Judge Bruce Schroeder upheld the objection, creating a notable moment in the highly publicised proceedings and highlighting judicial caution regarding AI-driven image manipulation.

During cross-examination, prosecutor Thomas Binger zoomed in on drone footage using an iPad to emphasise a detail for the jury. Defence attorney Mark Richards objected immediately, claiming that Apple's pinch-to-zoom function relies on AI to modify video, meaning the enlarged image would not represent the original, "virginal" state of the evidence.

Binger dismissed the claim, comparing zooming to using a magnifying glass and asserting it does not compromise the video's integrity. He noted that both sides had previously used enlarged images without issue. Judge Schroeder sided with the defence, rejecting the magnifying glass analogy. He required the prosecution to prove that zooming would not distort the video and requested expert testimony. However, they could not provide an expert on short notice.

The prosecution abandoned the live Zoom feature and presented the unaltered footage instead. Later, a state crime lab analyst testified about enlarged images created with professional software, allowing the defence to scrutinise the process.

This case attracted widespread media coverage and underscored growing concerns about the justice system's technical literacy in handling digital evidence. Experts noted that this incident reflects a recurring challenge in criminal trials: limited understanding of technology can influence case outcomes. While many considered the defence's argument misleading, the exchange highlighted the urgent need for verifiable, technically sound methods of presenting digital media in courtrooms. Specifically, two key points:

1. *Burden of proof:* By requiring the prosecution to demonstrate the reliability of the technology, the judge signalled strong scepticism towards potential digital manipulation, possibly setting a precedent for similar evidentiary disputes.
2. *Defence strategy:* Although the defence's claim was technically questionable, it proved effective in preventing the jury from viewing a key piece of evidence in the manner the prosecution intended.

4.3.4 People v. Foreman: Deepfake Concerns in Audio Evidence (2020)

In *People v. Foreman*, 2020 IL App (2d) 180178 [18], a case involving first-degree murder and residential burglary, the defendant raised a novel argument regarding the authenticity of recorded communications. He claimed that his voice had been cloned and argued that "in the age of so-called deepfake videos and easily manipulated audio recordings, improperly authenticated recorded communications should be inherently suspect."

The Illinois Appellate Court rejected this argument, emphasising that technological advancements alone do not render all recordings unreliable. The court held that, in the absence of any evidence of tampering or manipulation in the specific case, there were no foundational issues with admitting the recordings. This ruling underscores a critical principle: while deepfake technology introduces legitimate concerns about evidential integrity, courts require concrete proof of alteration rather than speculative claims.

The case also highlights an emerging challenge for the justice system: balancing awareness of synthetic media risks with the need to avoid undermining established evidentiary standards. As deepfake technology becomes more sophisticated, similar arguments are likely to surface, prompting courts to develop clearer guidelines for authentication and admissibility.

4.3.5 Matter of Weber: Generative AI and Expert Testimony (2024)

Although the following case was heard in a civil rather than criminal court, it provides valuable insight into the judiciary's emerging approach to AI and deepfake evidence. The dispute in *Matter of Weber* arose from a trust accounting conflict between Susan F. Weber, acting as trustee and executrix, and Owen K. Weber, the beneficiary. Owen alleged that Susan breached her fiduciary duty by mismanaging trust assets, including a property located in the Bahamas. To support his claim of lost profits, Owen engaged an expert witness, Mr Ranson, to estimate the hypothetical future value had the property been sold and the proceeds reinvested in the stock market. During testimony, it emerged that Mr Ranson had relied on Microsoft Copilot, a generative AI tool, to perform these calculations.

On 10 October 2024, the New York Surrogate's Court issued a landmark decision in the "Matter of Weber" (2024 NY Slip Op 24258), excluding the expert's testimony because it was based on outputs generated by Copilot. The court found this problematic due to the lack of transparency, repeatability, and understanding of how the AI reached its conclusions. The expert could not reproduce the outputs or recall the prompts used, and the court noted that the AI produced inconsistent results when queried multiple times.

This ruling underscores that AI-generated outputs (particularly from probabilistic models) do not meet the standards of reliability and verifiability required for expert evidence. It sets an important precedent for disclosure and validation when AI tools are used in legal proceedings.

The court excluded the expert's testimony and issued a strong caution regarding the use of generative AI in evidentiary contexts, noting the following:

- *Methodology could not be explained:* The expert could not explain how the AI tool worked, what data sources it used, or how it arrived at its output. When the calculation was replicated on a different device, it produced an inconsistent result, highlighting the tool's unreliability.
- *Probabilistic versus verifiable evidence:* The court emphasised that AI tools like Copilot are based on probabilistic models and are fundamentally unsuitable for precise financial calculations that demand verifiable, transparent, and reproducible methodologies.

The decision underscores that expert witnesses who rely on AI without validating its outputs risk having their credibility and judgment called into question.

4.3.6 Forgeries in Family Law

Personal litigation, particularly family proceedings, is highly susceptible to the use of altered evidence. Even though deliberately or recklessly misleading the court can result in contempt charges, fines, or even imprisonment, attempts to distort the truth are frequently uncovered (e.g. often in efforts to conceal wealth during divorce disputes).

One of the earliest and most striking examples of digital manipulation in family law occurred in 2020, when a mother attempted to persuade the court that the father was violent and dangerous by producing a doctored audio recording. The clip (edited using online software and tutorials) appeared to contain threats from the father. The tampering was only discovered through forensic analysis of the file's metadata, underscoring how easily accessible tools can be weaponised to fabricate evidence [19, 20].

High-profile cases have also demonstrated the lengths to which parties will go to mislead the court. In the widely reported *Akhmedova v Akhmedov* litigation [21], an international divorce spanning five jurisdictions, the Russian husband (worth over £1 billion) sought to shield assets, including a £250 million superyacht, from his wife. He even produced forged documents claiming the couple had already divorced in Russia. Although the wife was awarded £453 million, enforcement has proven elusive, with only around 10% recovered to date [20].

Other examples include *X v. Y* [2022] EWFC 95, where the financial remedy judgment in which the wife's capital claims were adjourned for a decade in view of dishonest fabrication of bank statements and uncertainty as to assets. The husband fabricated bank statements to convince his wife to relocate to England, promising financial security based on a fictional £80 million business sale. Once in England, the wife was left destitute, relying on state support [22, 23].

Similarly, in *Vispute v. Vispute* (2023), the wife altered bank statements during financial disclosure to misrepresent her income. The court found beyond reasonable doubt that her conduct amounted to interference with the due administration of justice, leading to a suspended four-month committal order [24]. In another case, a husband's falsified HSBC statements were exposed through document properties and a glaring error, referencing "31 September" [22].

While presenting forged or misleading evidence is not new, technological advances have made detection far more challenging. Most practitioners are familiar with "simple" forgeries (faked signatures, altered bank statements, or selectively edited WhatsApp messages) typically uncovered through inconsistencies in oral testimony, metadata analysis, or forensic expertise. However, the emergence of sophisticated digital fakes now threatens to undermine the credibility of litigants themselves. Deepfake audio and video, e.g. can fabricate threats, create false alibis, or distort character assessments, raising profound evidential risks.

The consequences for those who attempt to mislead the court remain severe, ranging from contempt of court to criminal prosecution. Recent legislative reforms, such as the UK Online Safety Act, have introduced new offences for creating doctored, sexually explicit images of adults, with penalties including unlimited fines. Yet these consequences only apply when media manipulation is detected, which is a growing challenge as synthetic media becomes more convincing and harder to trace.

4.3.7 Emerging Trends

Legal professionals caution that the use of synthetic media in litigation is poised to become a major challenge. Defendants may increasingly introduce deepfake videos or audio recordings to fabricate timelines or create misleading narratives, complicating the authentication of evidence. This tactic has already surfaced in pretrial discovery disputes, where parties have attempted to leverage AI-generated content to undermine opposing claims [16]. The trend signals a growing need for courts to adopt rigorous standards for verifying digital media and to develop protocols that address the unique risks posed by generative AI in evidentiary contexts.

There are a growing range of technologies that can be used in the defence against fake evidence, e.g.:

- *Imagery and video:* Amped Five can be used to identify the processing history behind images and videos.

- *Audio:* Pindrop (and similar solutions), which is used in the financial services sector, can help with the detection of audio deepfakes, looking at several factors including reverberation, compression, and transcoding.
- *Financial documents:* Resistant AI (which offers over 500 detectors in the analysis of forged documents) can identify falsified evidence in financial documents, which the human eye is often unable to detect.

Additionally, the University of York's "Deepfakes as Forensic Evidence" project addresses the growing challenge of synthetic audio in criminal investigations. Its primary goal is to develop robust methodologies for forensic voice comparison by identifying linguistic and phonetic markers that differentiate genuine speech from AI-generated imitations. This research fills a critical gap in forensic science, where deepfake audio threatens evidential integrity and admissibility in court. By creating validated detection frameworks and integrating them into forensic workflows, the project aims to strengthen the justice system's ability to counter audio-based deception and maintain trust in digital evidence [25].

Deepfakes have introduced a range of evidentiary challenges that are reshaping the landscape of digital forensics and legal practice. Issues such as the reproducibility of AI-generated outputs, the lack of transparency in detection tools, and the complexities surrounding the chain of custody raise serious concerns about the reliability and admissibility of digital evidence. Moreover, the existence of deepfake technology itself enables plausible deniability, allowing individuals to dispute genuine audiovisual evidence by claiming it has been fabricated. These challenges not only complicate forensic investigations but also threaten the integrity of judicial processes.

There is still limited clarity regarding how courts will handle deepfake evidence or the extent to which it may affect trial outcomes. Although only a small number of cases have involved deepfake allegations so far, the available examples reveal strikingly inconsistent judicial responses. This reality underscores the urgent need for courts and legal practitioners to establish clear rules and procedures for assessing authenticity when deepfake involvement is suspected. Developing robust standards for verification will be critical to maintaining evidential integrity and ensuring fair trials.

4.4 Summary

Manipulated media, particularly deepfakes, is increasingly being used in ways that obstruct justice and complicate forensic investigations. Criminal applications such as fraud, extortion, and harassment exploit synthetic audio and video to deceive victims and authorities. When deepfakes are introduced as evidence, they challenge traditional forensic protocols and courtroom standards, raising concerns about authenticity, admissibility, and the reliability of detection methods. High-profile cases have demonstrated how convincingly altered media can delay investigations, mislead legal proceedings, and erode public trust in digital evidence. These issues highlight the urgent need for forensic and legal systems to adapt to the evolving threat of synthetic media, creating policies on AI usage and deepfake detection.

References

[1] J. Burton, A. Janjeva, and S. Moseley, 'AI and serious online crime', CETaS Research Reports, Centre for Emerging Technology and Security (CETaS), The Alan Turing Institute, London, UK, Research Report, Mar. 2025. Available: https://cetas.turing.ac.uk/sites/default/files/2025-03/cetas_research_report_-_ai_and_serious_online_crime_0.pdf.

[2] Europol, 'Facing reality? Law enforcement and the challenge of deepfakes – An observatory report from Europol Innovation Lab', Luxembourg, 2022. doi: 10.2813/158794.

[3] Interpol, 'Beyond illusions: Unmasking the threat of synthetic media for law enforcement', Lyon, June 2024. Available: www.interpol.int/en/News-and-Events/News/2024/Beyond-illusions-Unmasking-the-threat-of-synthetic-media-for-law-enforcement.

[4] S. He, Y. Lei, Z. Zhang, Y. Sun, S. Li, C. Zhang, and J. Ye, 'Identity deepfake threats to biometric authentication systems: public and expert perspectives', Jun. 2025. Available: http://arxiv.org/abs/2506.06825

[5] We Protect Global Alliance, *New film exposes AI's role in online child sexual exploitation and calls for urgent global action*, We Protect Global Alliance. London, UK. Jan. 2026

[6] M. Redley, 'Department of Education takes bold step to tackle new era of misinformation', *SECNewgate*. Available: www.secnewgate.co.uk/our-insights/department-education-takes-bold-step-tackle-new-era-misinformation.

[7] S. Alanazi and S. Asif, 'Exploring deepfake technology: creation, consequences and countermeasures', *Human-Intelligent Systems Integration*, vol. 6, no. 1, pp. 49–60, Dec. 2024, doi: 10.1007/s42454-024-00054-8.

[8] S. Ahmed, M. Masood, A. W. T. Bee, and K. Ichikawa, 'False failures, real distrust: The impact of an infrastructure failure deepfake on government trust', *Frontiers in Psychology*, vol. 16, 2025, doi: 10.3389/fpsyg.2025.1574840.

[9] S. A. Laczi and V. Poser, 'Impact of deepfake technology on children: Risks and consequences', in *SISY 2024 – IEEE 22nd International Symposium on Intelligent Systems and Informatics, Proceedings*, Institute of Electrical and Electronics Engineers Inc., 2024, pp. 215–220. doi: 10.1109/SISY62279.2024.10737593.

[10] M. N. A. Latif Al Waroi, 'False reality: Deepfakes in terrorist propaganda', *Security Intelligence Terrorism Journal (SITJ)*, vol. 1, no. 1, pp. 41–59, Aug. 2024.

[11] J. Hörnle, 'Deepfakes and the law: Why Britain needs stronger protections against technology-facilitated abuse', School of Law, Queen Mary University of London. Available: www.qmul.ac.uk/law/news/2025/items/deepfakes-and-the-law-why-britain-needs-stronger-protections-against-technology-facilitated-abuse.html.

[12] R. Satter, 'US teachers union says it is leaving X over sexualized AI images of children', *Reuters*. Available: www.reuters.com/business/media-telecom/teachers-union-says-its-leaving-x-calling-ai-images-children-the-last-straw-2026-01-13/.

[13] K. J. Quilty, 'Washington court rejects novel use of AI-enhanced video in trial', *GreenbergTrurig*. Available: www.gtlaw.com/-/media/files/insights/alerts/2024/05/gt-alert_washington-court-rejects-novel-use-of-ai-enhanced-video-in-trial.pdf?rev=21061be691c0410498ceb6148488e1b8.

[14] K. O. Jones and B. S. Jones, 'How robust is the United Kingdom justice system against the advance of deepfake audio and video?', in *Proceedings of the 36th International Conference on Information Technologies (InfoTech-2022)*, Bulgaria: IEEE, Sep. 2022, pp. 13–24.

[15] J. Perlo, 'AI-generated evidence is showing up in court. Judges say they're not ready', *NBC News*. Available: www.nbcnews.com/tech/tech-news/ai-generated-evidence-deepfake-use-law-judges-object-rcna235976.

[16] J. M. Loring, G. H. Ryan, and J. Walker, 'Synthetic media creates new authenticity concerns for legal evidence', *The National Law Review*. Available: https://natlawreview.com/article/synthetic-media-creates-new-authenticity-concerns-legal-evidence.

[17] A. Mitchell, 'Deepfaked evidence: What case law tells us about how the rules of authenticity needs to change', California, Jun. 2025.

[18] S. D. Illinois Appellate Court, 'People v. Foreman, 2020 IL App (2d) 180178', Illinois, Jul. 2020.

[19] CYFOR (2020), Deepfake audio evidence used in UK court to discredit father. Available: https://cyfor.co.uk/deepfake-audio-evidence-used-in-uk-court-to-discredit-father/.

[20] The National News (2020), Deepfake audio evidence used in UK court to discredit Dubai dad. Available: https://www.thenationalnews.com/uae/courts/deepfake-audio-evidence-used-in-uk-court-to-discredit-dubai-dad-1.975764.

[21] UK Courts and Tribunals Judiciary, 'Akhmedova -v- Akhmedova and ors – [2021] EWHC 545 (Fam)', England and Wales High Court (Family Division).

[22] R. Dziobon and E. Moodey, 'From photoshop to deepfakes: The evolution of fake evidence creation in family law cases', Penningtons Manches Cooper LLP, *Insight Article*, London, Sept 2024. Available: www.penningtonslaw.com/insights/from-photoshop-to-deepfakes-the-evolution-of-fake-evidence-creation-in-family-law-cases/.

[23] P. Morgan, 'X v Y [2022] EWFC 95', *Financial Remedies Journal*. Available: https://financialremediesjournal.com/x-v-y-2022-ewfc-95/.

[24] UK Judiciary, 'Vispute v Vispute RCJ Family Division Judgement', London, Apr. 2023.

[25] University of York, 'Deepfakes as forensic evidence', YorVoice Project. Available: www.york.ac.uk/research/sparks/yorvoice/deepfakes-forensic-evidence/.

5

Challenges for Digital Forensics and Law Enforcement

The growing prevalence of deepfakes and AI-generated media presents significant challenges for digital forensic professionals and law enforcement agencies. As synthetic content becomes more convincing and accessible, investigators face mounting obstacles in identifying, verifying, and managing manipulated media and evidence. These challenges extend beyond technical detection, encompassing procedural concerns such as maintaining chain of custody, ensuring evidentiary admissibility, and responding to plausible deniability in court. Real-world use cases (from fraud and harassment, to misinformation and identity theft) highlight the urgent need for updated forensic protocols, cross-disciplinary training, and legal reform. This chapter explores the multifaceted difficulties encountered by police and DFUs, examining the intersection of technology, investigative practice, and judicial scrutiny in the age of synthetic media.

5.1 Challenges for the Policing Sector and Digital Forensic Units

Nearly 90% of criminal cases now involve digital evidence analysis, and the sheer volume of items of interest (ranging from device logs and cloud data to multimedia artefacts) continues to grow exponentially. This surge places immense pressure on forensic units, contributing to significant case backlogs and delays in judicial processes [1]. The introduction of deepfakes and other forms of fabricated media further complicates this landscape, adding layers of complexity to evidence authentication and chain-of-custody verification. Deepfake creation tools have become increasingly accessible, enabling individuals

 DOI: 10.1201/9781003714811-5

with little technical expertise to produce highly convincing forgeries. At the same time, the gap between the sophistication of deepfake generation and the effectiveness of detection technologies continues to widen.

With deepfake-related crimes having surged by over 300% since 2019, the need for robust investigative frameworks and advanced forensic capabilities has never been more urgent [2]. Fraud is evolving at an unprecedented pace, shifting from amateur phishing kits to sophisticated, fraud-as-a-service (FaaS) platforms. Criminals are exploiting automation and social engineering to stay ahead of the curve, making the challenge more complex than ever (Figure 5.1).

As a result, DFUs and law enforcement agencies must constantly adapt to evolving techniques and tools used in synthetic media creation, ensuring they remain equipped to preserve evidential integrity in an era of pervasive digital manipulation.

5.1.1 Skills Gap in Detecting Deepfake and Fabricated Media

Many DFUs face a significant skills gap, with a noticeable lack of awareness around digital manipulation via AI and deepfakes. While frontline officers increasingly have access to tools for basic data extraction, and investigators are tasked with reviewing outputs from forensic analyses, they often encounter diverse sources of digital evidence whose relevance may not be immediately clear. This lack of contextual understanding can lead to missed opportunities for timely intervention. A critical concern is the growing lack of awareness of how easily and convincingly deepfake media can be created using publicly available tools and the myriad number of ways these could be used within crimes or presented as evidence [4, 5].

This knowledge gap within policing communities can hinder timely recognition and response, allowing manipulated content to influence cases before its authenticity is questioned -underscoring the need for structured training. Currently, there is no national digital forensics training program, in the UK, nor a globally recognised equivalent, leaving practitioners without standardised guidance on identifying and interpreting complex fabricated and deepfake digital evidence [6].

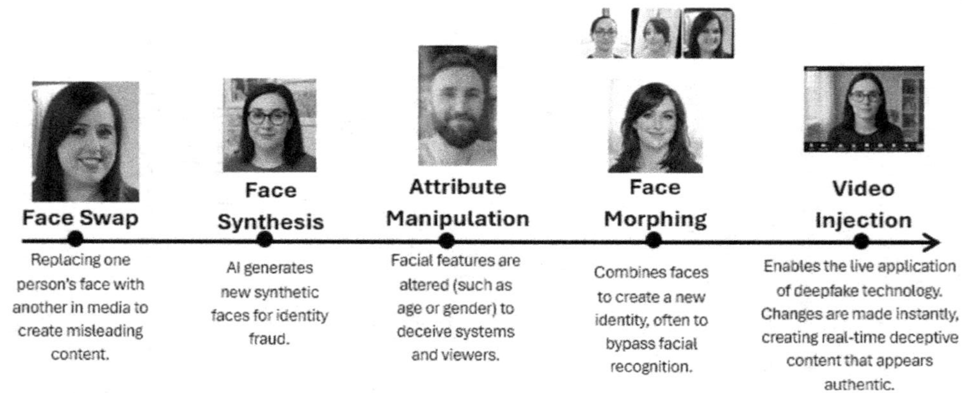

Figure 5.1 Industrialisation of deepfake fraud created by GPT 5.0 [3]. Created using elements from the Face Swap image in Figure 2.2 Remaker AI v2, with additional AI-based face morphing/attribute manipulation using the author's own images. AI Tool Attribution: Includes AI-generated face morphing/attribute manipulation based on author-provided images. Face synthesis Image: Imaged generated using Copilot with the prompt: could you create face synthesis based on images provided…remove the Disney ears. AI Tool Attribution: Image generated using M365 Copilot (GPT-5). Attribute Manipulation Image generated using a real photograph and ChatGPT with the prompt: could you edit this photo, by changing the colour of his beard and making it slightly longer…brown and noticeably longer… Add hair to his head" - OpenAI. (2026). ChatGPT (GPT-5.3) [AI image generator]. Face Morphing Image generated using ChatGPT with the prompt: create a new photo merging these three faces (it is for an illustration) – OpenAI. (2026). ChatGPT (GPT-5.3) [AI image generator]. Video Injection Image generated using M365 Copilot (GPT-5) with the prompt: create an image of a person's face in an online Zoom meeting. AI Tool Attribution: Image generated using M365 Copilot (GPT-5).

5.1.2 Resource Constraints

Law enforcement agencies are increasingly challenged by limited resources; both in terms of budget and access to advanced detection tools. Many investigative units lack the infrastructure needed to keep pace with a rapidly evolving threat landscape. This problem is compounded by the growing complexity of authentication and verification processes, particularly when dealing with fabricated media such as deepfakes. In addition, identifying and analysing deepfakes can be highly labour-intensive, requiring meticulous scrutiny and cross-verification. These steps, while essential for accuracy, significantly slow investigations and reduce operational efficiency. As a result, agencies face critical time constraints that must now be factored into their workflows.

Authenticating digital evidence has become significantly more time-consuming than in the past. Tasks that once took minutes can now require hours, due to multilayered verification protocols. Take surveillance footage as an example: previously, investigators could quickly assess its authenticity and move forward. Today, that same footage must undergo rigorous scrutiny, including processing through specialised deepfake detection tools, expert review by digital forensic analysts, and meticulous documentation at every stage. What was once a 30-minute exercise can easily stretch into a full-day operation. In time-sensitive investigations, these delays can critically affect case progression and resource allocation. This challenge is further compounded by the lack of repeatability in results and the need to employ multiple tools to confirm whether content has been manipulated.

5.1.3 Trust in Digital Media

Until recently, participants in the judicial process operated under a shared belief that "video doesn't lie." This foundational assumption allowed law enforcement to develop streamlined procedures for managing digital evidence, with verification efforts focused primarily on maintaining a secure chain of custody rather than scrutinising the content itself [7]. However, the rise of deepfakes has fundamentally disrupted this paradigm. Today, every piece of digital evidence must now undergo rigorous authentication. Unfortunately, most midsize police departments lack the technological infrastructure and investigative protocols necessary to support this level of scrutiny. The shift from viewing digital media as inherently trustworthy to treating it with caution represents one of the most profound procedural changes in modern investigative practice [7].

Looking ahead, law enforcement agencies face an escalating challenge: preserving the integrity of criminal investigations in an era where verifying the authenticity of digital evidence is increasingly complex. In some cases, crimes may arise directly from deepfakes or related misinformation. Here, officers must not only conduct the criminal investigation but also verify the authenticity of the media and determine whether the content is genuine or fabricated.

To meet this challenge, agencies must adapt their investigative approaches, invest in specialised training, and integrate advanced media verification tools into their workflows.

5.1.4 Legislation and Policy Limitations

Deepfakes are increasingly disrupting DFUs and cyber investigations by introducing complex challenges in evidence validation, media authentication, and maintaining investigative integrity. International bodies such as Interpol [8], Europol [2], and Homeland Security [9, 10] have issued warnings about the growing risks and misuse potential of deepfake and fabricated media. Despite these alerts, a significant gap in operational readiness persists, particularly within the UK. While the identification of deepfakes in active investigations is still emerging, the frequency of manipulated media encounters is rising, yet awareness of appropriate forensic methodologies and handling protocols remains low.

This lack of preparedness is compounded by the absence of formal guidance or legislation from employers and regulatory authorities, leaving DFUs without clear frameworks for responding to deepfake-related incidents. As manipulated media becomes increasingly prevalent in investigations, awareness of appropriate forensic methodologies and handling protocols remains limited. Consequently, there is an urgent need to establish and disseminate best practice guidelines and forensic methodologies tailored to the unique challenges posed by AI-generated forgeries. Such measures are essential to uphold evidential integrity and maintain reliability in an era of increasingly convincing synthetic media.

Further exacerbating these challenges are significant attribution and jurisdictional barriers. Identifying perpetrators is difficult because generators can anonymise themselves, spoof identities, and operate across borders, while the proliferation of open-source tools further reduces forensic traceability. As a result, very few cases lead to successful attribution. Cross-jurisdictional enforcement adds another layer of complexity, as laws differ widely between countries. These combined gaps in preparedness, guidance, and enforcement mean that deepfake crimes often go unpunished, underscoring the critical need for coordinated international policy and robust forensic standards [2, 4, 8, 9, 11].

5.2 Technical Challenges in Detecting Deepfakes

Detecting deepfakes remains a highly complex task due to rapid advancements in generative technologies and the limitations of current forensic tools. Several key challenges contribute to this difficulty:

- *Absence or manipulation of digital fingerprints:* Authentic media typically contains identifiable traces such as metadata, compression signatures, and device-specific fingerprints. Deepfakes, however, may lack these markers or deliberately mimic legitimate signals, rendering conventional provenance tracking unreliable.
- *Increasingly sophisticated generative models:* Modern techniques (such as GANs and diffusion models) evolve rapidly, producing highly realistic outputs that challenge existing detection systems. Continuous updates are essential to keep pace with these advancements.
- *Reduction of visual artefacts:* Early deepfakes exhibited noticeable flaws (e.g. unnatural blinking, inconsistent lighting). Contemporary methods have largely eliminated these artefacts, making traditional anomaly-based detection approaches far less effective.
- *Multimodal manipulation:* Deepfakes often involve both audio and video alterations, yet many detection tools focus on a single modality. Ensuring synchronisation between modalities (i.e. lip movements and speech) remains technically challenging and underexplored.
- *Generalisation limitations:* Current deepfake detection models often suffer from overfitting, making them less effective when encountering previously unseen or out-of-distribution

deepfakes. Despite progress in addressing this issue, the rapid evolution of generative techniques ensures that generalisation remains a persistent challenge.

- *Linguistic diversity challenges:* Most detection methods prioritise English, neglecting other languages. Developing multilingual datasets and language-agnostic features is critical, particularly for approaches relying on speech patterns or lip-sync accuracy. Without this, language-specific cues essential for detection remain underutilised.
- *Inconsistent tool outputs and lack of benchmarking:* Different forensic tools often produce conflicting results, and the absence of standardised benchmarks makes it difficult to validate performance or establish trust in detection outcomes.
- *Adversarial attacks:* Deepfake creators can deliberately introduce changes that evade detection, like slight noise perturbations or watermark removal. Detection models can be fooled, leading to both false negatives and reduced trust in forensic analysis.

5.2.1 Limitations of Existing Forensic Tools

Despite advancements in detection technologies, current forensic tools face significant limitations that undermine their reliability in real-world investigations.

- *Narrow focus on AI manipulation:* Most detectors are designed to identify signs of generative AI manipulation but overlook traditional editing techniques such as splicing, recontextualisation, or subtle frame alterations. This results in incomplete assessments of media authenticity.
- *Results are probabilistic, not definitive:* Detection tools vary widely in accuracy, often produce ambiguous outputs, and rarely provide clear explanations of their findings. As demonstrated in Chapters 2 and 5, relying solely on these tools is insufficient for robust forensic analysis. Human judgement and contextual analysis are still essential.
- *Binary classification issues:* Many tools frame detection as a simple "AI-generated or not" decision, often producing probabilistic outputs like *undetermined* or *uncertain*. There is often no clear explanation of why it was flagged. Such ambiguity

is problematic in forensic and legal contexts where definitive conclusions are required.

- *Inconsistent results and reproducibility:* Detection outcomes vary based on media resolution, compression, manipulation type, and even system environment. Some AI-based detectors produce different results across repeated tests, undermining reproducibility – a critical requirement for courtroom admissibility.

A recent study by the Commonwealth Scientific and Industrial Research Organisation (CSIRO), an Australian Government agency responsible for scientific research, and South Korea's Sungkyunkwan University evaluated 16 top deepfake detectors and found that none could consistently identify deepfakes in real-world scenarios. Each of the detectors had major flaws leading to false positives, false negatives, and general confusion [12, 13].

As highlighted in Chapter 4, there is a notable lack of clarity regarding correct legal rulings and the various ways deepfakes or AI-generated manipulations can be introduced into proceedings. Judges may preside over cases involving AI fraud or deepfakes without sufficient knowledge to make informed decisions. The examples illustrate significant cases with differing rulings and defence strategies.

5.2.2 Data Challenges in Deepfake Detection

Developing robust deepfake detection models is significantly hindered by a range of data-related challenges that affect both performance and generalisability.

- *Lack of standardisation and evaluation metrics:* No universal frameworks exist for evaluating deepfake detection models, making cross-study comparisons unreliable.

  This makes it difficult to compare results across studies and can lead to misleading conclusions about model effectiveness. Many models report high accuracy under ideal conditions yet struggle when applied to low quality or compressed media (formats commonly encountered on social media platforms where deepfakes are frequently shared).
- *Dataset imbalance:* Many datasets are skewed towards either fake or real samples and lack variation in subjects, lighting,

backgrounds, and manipulation techniques, reducing real-world applicability.

- *Overfitting:* Detection models often learn dataset-specific artefacts rather than genuine indicators of manipulation, making them ineffective against newer, more sophisticated deepfakes.
- *Media differences:* Detecting deepfakes is harder in photos than in videos because videos provide temporal cues (eye blinking, head motion, lip sync). Images lack motion-based inconsistencies; as a result, single-image detection is often unreliable.

Together, these technical, forensic, and data-related challenges highlight the urgent need for adaptive detection strategies, standardised evaluation protocols, and comprehensive forensic frameworks. Without these, law enforcement and digital forensic units will struggle to maintain evidential integrity and investigative reliability in the face of increasingly convincing synthetic media.

5.3 Forensic Readiness in an Era of AI-Driven Crime

The growing complexity of digital crime- particularly involving deepfakes and synthetic media- has exposed a significant technological divide across law enforcement agencies. Small and midsize police departments frequently operate within constrained resource environments, lacking the substantial funding and technical infrastructure available to larger metropolitan forces, yet facing the same sophisticated threats including AI-generated NCII, CSAM, impersonation, fraud, and evidence tampering that demand advanced forensic capabilities.

The prevalence of fabricated and deepfake media in forensic investigations is rising, with manipulated content increasingly appearing in cases involving fraud, harassment, and identity theft. Crucially, confirming the authenticity of suspect deepfake material is considerably more time-consuming than traditional media verification — a challenge compounded by the variable availability and accuracy of detection tools, which can differ widely in performance depending on an agency's resources and technical expertise.

As digital evidence becomes central to a growing number of investigations, demand for forensic data analysis has surged. According to the Office for National Statistics, over 4.2 million fraud offences were recorded in the UK in the year ending March 2025 (a 31% increase compared to the previous year) making fraud the largest category of headline crime [14]. Many of these cases involve digital forensic analysis, and according to the Crown Prosecution Service, digital device examination now plays a role in the majority of criminal investigations, particularly those involving cyber-enabled offences such as harassment, identity theft, and financial fraud.

The evolving landscape of digital forensics, and the growing detection and authentication challenges posed by deepfakes and AI will likely require substantial investment to keep pace with emerging threats. Fortunately, several federal and national funding programmes (including targeted grants for technology upgrades and training) offer support to help alleviate financial pressures associated with implementing deepfake detection and digital evidence authentication systems [7].

Beyond funding, a significant knowledge gap persists across the sector. Many forensic examiners and frontline officers remain unaware of the full capabilities of deepfake creation and detection tools. Increasing awareness and providing targeted training on synthetic media manipulation techniques is essential for improving investigative response times and ensuring accurate identification of manipulated content [15].

Addressing these issues demands not only financial investment but also coordinated strategic planning, cross-agency and cross-sector collaboration, and a sustained commitment to upskilling personnel at all levels of law enforcement. Researchers and academic scholars have already played an important role in advancing understanding in this area, helping bridge the gap between practice and emerging threat landscapes, and fostering more joined-up dialogue and collaboration across the field.

5.3.1 Deepfake Practitioner Insight Survey (2025)

A 2025 study conducted by Liverpool John Moores University gathered insights from digital forensic practitioners and researchers worldwide [4]. The primary objective was to assess the prevalence of cases involving deepfake or fabricated media and evaluate the level of preparedness within the field. The findings reinforce the view that deepfakes and synthetic media constitute an emerging threat, necessitating greater attention, targeted training, and the development of specialised tools within digital forensic and cybersecurity workflows. Notably, 86% of respondents indicated that their employer either lacked guidance or legislation on deepfakes (or that they are unaware of such measures). This absence of formal direction suggests that many professionals are addressing the challenges posed by synthetic media without structured support, policies, or training. Consequently, there is an urgent need for organisations to establish clear protocols, educational resources, and legal frameworks to enable practitioners to respond effectively to deepfake-related incidents.

The study also revealed strong community consensus on the importance of rigorous forensic standards to ensure evidence reliability and admissibility. Yet practitioners face a critical gap: the lack of formalised guidance and universally accepted protocols. In the absence of established frameworks, many rely on ad hoc/trial-and-error approaches, resulting in inconsistencies in methodology and outcomes. This gap underscores the pressing need for collaborative efforts to develop standardised procedures, particularly as the complexity and frequency of deepfake cases continue to rise.

A recurring theme was the shortage of tools and standards. Respondents expressed concern over the absence of industry-approved tools and the need for standardised methodologies for detecting and managing deepfakes. This issue was frequently linked to a perceived gap in both research literature and practical guidance, highlighting the necessity for more structured and systematic approaches within the field. Concerns were also raised about interpreting detection results and understanding the significance of output data, alongside growing apprehension regarding the transparency and reliability of explainable AI.

When asked which sectors are most vulnerable to deepfake-related threats, respondents identified several high-risk industries. Finance emerged as a primary concern, largely due to the potential for fraud, impersonation, and financial manipulation. Media and politics were also frequently cited, reflecting growing anxieties around misinformation, fake news, and reputational harm. Government was highlighted as well, particularly in connection with national security risks, disinformation campaigns, and the possibility of diplomatic sabotage.

Healthcare, e-commerce, and retail were noted for their exposure to identity fraud and customer impersonation. Additional sectors mentioned (including law enforcement, education, digital forensics, insurance, infrastructure, entertainment, and the military) appeared across multiple responses, suggesting broad recognition of deepfake-related vulnerabilities. Less commonly cited but still relevant were marketing, technology, and social media. Overall, the responses indicate that deepfake threats are perceived as cross-sectoral, with heightened concern for industries that handle sensitive data, public-facing communications, or financial transactions [11].

5.3.2 Interpretability, Reproducibility, and Explainability

The integration of AI and deep learning tools into digital forensics and policing introduces critical challenges around interpretability, reproducibility, and explainability – issues that directly affect evidentiary integrity and legal admissibility. Investigators operate under strict procedural guidelines (such as those outlined by ACPO), requiring every action on digital evidence to be fully documented and justified. As identified, many AI models, particularly deep learning systems, produce outputs without transparent reasoning, offering no clear account of how conclusions are reached.. This lack of interpretability makes it difficult to explain how a model reached its conclusion, an essential requirement in forensic workflows and courtroom settings. For instance, if a deepfake detection tool flags a video as manipulated, investigators must be able to trace and articulate the specific features or anomalies that informed that decision. Without such clarity, the output risks being dismissed as speculative or inadmissible.

Reproducibility poses an equally significant challenge. Deepfake detectors and AI-based forensic tools must deliver consistent results across identical inputs and environments to be considered reliable. However, many open-source and proprietary detection systems lack standardised testing protocols, often producing different scores or classifications for the same media depending on system configuration, model version, or runtime conditions. This variability undermines confidence in the tool's robustness and raises serious concerns about its use in legal proceedings. Further complicating matters is the absence of transparency around model architecture, training data, and update cycles, making it difficult for forensic experts to validate or defend the tool's reliability under cross-examination.

Explainability (supported by advances in Explainable AI (XAI)) is essential to bridge the gap between technical complexity and legal accountability. XAI techniques aim to make AI decisions interpretable by highlighting which features influenced a model's output and how. In forensic contexts, this enables investigators to present clear, structured reasoning behind AI-generated findings. Tools such as *Magnet Verify* illustrate how explainability can be operationalised, performing structural analysis of media files, identifying manipulation, and providing traceable, human-readable outputs that support evidentiary presentation. These capabilities not only enhance the usability of AI tools in real-world investigations but also strengthen their admissibility and credibility in court.

Ultimately, integrating AI into digital forensics (particularly for detecting and analysing deepfake or AI-generated content) requires a cautious and principled approach. AI systems must prioritise transparency, ensuring their methods and decision-making processes are understandable to forensic practitioners, legal professionals, and other stakeholders. Reproducibility is equally critical: independent experts should be able to replicate analyses and verify findings, given the high stakes of legal proceedings. Furthermore, compliance with legal, ethical, and evidentiary standards is essential to safeguard privacy, uphold due process, and meet admissibility requirements in court.

Procedural rigour must also be maintained through meticulous documentation of workflows, algorithms, and data sources, so that detection tools and any AI-assisted conclusions about media authenticity can withstand scrutiny. As deepfake and AI technologies evolve rapidly, forensic teams must remain vigilant about the limitations and potential biases of AI tools, clearly communicating any uncertainties in their analyses. Without these safeguards, AI risks producing evidence that is misleading, unverifiable, or legally indefensible; undermining trust in forensic outcomes rather than enhancing investigative capabilities.

Moreover, law enforcement agencies and DFUs face additional challenges when presenting deepfake or AI-generated content as evidence in court. Such evidence must be forensically sound, collected and analysed using rigorous methods that can withstand scrutiny and be independently verified. Analysts must present findings with precision, ensuring that conclusions about authenticity or manipulation are accurate, objective, and grounded in verifiable facts. Given the complexity and novelty of AI-generated media, clarity and adherence to accepted forensic standards are paramount to convey truth without exaggeration or ambiguity. Table 5.1 summarises these key points.

Table 5.1 Deepfake Detection Challenges and Mitigation Strategies

CHALLENGE	DESCRIPTION	POTENTIAL MITIGATION STRATEGIES
Evidence Integrity and Admissibility	Difficulty verifying authenticity of media, and risk of evidence being inadmissible in court.	- Use forensically sound acquisition and analysis methods - Document processes for reproducibility and explainability - Employ multiple detection tools and cross-verify results
Rapid Technological Evolution	Deepfake tools evolve faster than detection methods	- Continuous training of detection models with updated datasets - Collaborate with research institutions and AI labs – Implement adaptive detection pipelines that can incorporate new techniques
Resource and Skill Constraints	Limited personnel with expertise in AI and deepfake forensics	- Specialised training programs for police officers and DFUs - Use user-friendly AI tools with clear workflows
Public Misinformation and Trust	Deepfakes can spread disinformation, complicating investigations	- Public awareness campaigns on AI-generated content - Rapid verification protocols for viral content - Transparent communication about investigations and AI use
Attribution Challenges	Difficulty in identifying creators of deepfakes	- Develop investigative frameworks combining AI detection with metadata analysis - Collaborate with cybersecurity experts and platform providers - Leverage blockchain or digital watermarking for provenance tracking

CHALLENGE	DESCRIPTION	POTENTIAL MITIGATION STRATEGIES
Legal and Ethical Considerations	Laws on AI-generated content and evidence are still evolving	- Develop internal guidelines for AI use in investigations - Ensure compliance with privacy laws - Consult legal teams before deploying AI forensic tools
Scalability and Automation	Large volumes of content require automated detection, risking false positives/negatives	- Implement human-in-the-loop verification systems - Prioritise high-risk content for detailed analysis - Continuously evaluate AI tool performance against benchmarks

5.4 Summary

The rise of deepfakes and other forms of fabricated media presents complex challenges for digital forensics and law enforcement. Traditional investigative techniques, which rely on the authenticity of digital evidence, are increasingly undermined by synthetic content that is difficult to detect and easy to disseminate. Forensic practitioners face technical hurdles in developing reliable detection tools, procedural complexities in maintaining evidentiary integrity, and legal uncertainties surrounding admissibility in court. At the same time, law enforcement agencies must contend with the speed and scale at which manipulated media spreads, often fuelling misinformation, fraud, and social unrest. Addressing these challenges requires a multifaceted approach: combining advanced deepfake/AI-driven detection methods, robust forensic readiness frameworks, and international collaboration on policy and regulation. Without these measures, safeguarding truth and maintaining judicial integrity in the digital age will remain at risk.

References

[1] The Science and Technology Select Committee, 'Forensic science and the criminal justice system: A blueprint for change', London, May 2019. Available: https://publications.parliament.uk/pa/ld201719/ldselect/ldsctech/333/333.pdf.

[2] Europol, 'Facing reality? Law enforcement and the challenge of deepfakes – An Observatory Report from Europol Innovation Lab', Luxembourg, 2022. doi: 10.2813/158794.

[3] A. Lurie and T. Naor, 'Top fraud trends for 2024–2025', AU10TIX. Available: www.au10tix.com/blog/top-fraud-trends-for-2024-2025/.

[4] Á. MacDermott, 'Deepfake forensic survey dataset', Liverpool John Moores University. Dataset available via JISC. LJMU Ethics Approval Reference: 25/CMP/004., Oct. 2025.

[5] Á. MacDermott, 'Deepfake forensics: Exploring the impact and implications of fabricated media in digital forensic investigations – DFRWS EU poster', in *Digital Forensics Research Workshop Europe (DFRWS EU 2025). Brno, Czech Republic*, 2025. Accessed: Apr. 03, 2025. Available: https://dfrws.org/wp-content/uploads/2025/04/DFRWS_EU_2025_paperposter_115.pdf

[6] National Police Chief's Council (NPCC), 'Digital forensic science strategy', UK, Jul. 2020. Accessed: Aug. 11, 2024. Available: www.npcc.police.uk/SysSiteAssets/media/downloads/publications/publications-log/2020/national-digital-forensic-science-strategy.pdf

[7] K. Gomez, 'How deepfakes will challenge the future of digital evidence in law enforcement,' Police1, Apr. 15, 2025. Available: www.police1.com/investigations/how-deepfakes-will-challenge-the-future-of-digital-evidence-in-law-enforcement.

[8] Interpol, 'Beyond illusions: Unmasking the threat of synthetic media for law enforcement', Lyon, Jun. 2024. Available: www.interpol.int/en/News-and-Events/News/2024/Beyond-illusions-Unmasking-the-threat-of-synthetic-media-for-law-enforcement.

[9] Homeland Security, 'The increasing threat of deepfake identities', Washington, DC, Aug. 2021. Available: www.dhs.gov/sites/default/files/publications/increasing_threats_of_deepfake_identities_0.pdf.

[10] Homeland Security, 'Impact of artificial intelligence (AI) on criminal and illicit activities', Washington, DC, 2024. Available: www.dhs.gov/sites/default/files/2024-10/24_0927_ia_aep-impact-ai-on-criminal-and-illicit-activities.pdf.

[11] Á. MacDermott, 'Ctrl+Alt+deceit: Policing the deepfake dilemma', Forensic Science International: Digital Investigation, no. DFRWS EU 2026-Selected Papers from the 13th Annual Digital Forensics Research Conference Europe, Mar. 2026.

[12] CSIRO, 'Research reveals "major vulnerabilities" in deepfake detectors', Available: www.csiro.au/en/news/All/News/2025/March/Research-reveals-major-vulnerabilities-in-deepfake-detectors.

[13] B. M. Le, J. Kim, S. S. Woo, K. Moore, A. Abuadbba, and S. Tariq, 'SoK: Systematization and benchmarking of deepfake detectors in a unified framework', *ArXiv*, no. 2401.04364, Mar. 2025. Available: http://arxiv.org/abs/2401.04364

[14] UK Office for National Statistics, 'Crime in England and Wales: Year ending June 2025', Office for National Statistics. Available: www.ons.gov.uk/peoplepopulationandcommunity/crimeandjustice/bulletins/crimeinenglandandwales/yearendingjune2025.

[15] I. Amerini *et al.*, "Deepfake media forensics: Status and future challenges", *Journal of Imaging*, vol. 11, no. 3, Mar. 2025, doi: 10.3390/jimaging11030073.

6

Legal and Ethical Implications of Deepfake Technology

The proliferation of deepfake technology presents complex legal and ethical challenges that are reshaping the landscape of digital media and forensic investigation. As synthetic content becomes increasingly realistic and accessible, questions around the admissibility and reliability of deepfake evidence in court have come to the forefront. Legal systems must now address the difficulties with verifying the authenticity of digital media. At the same time, deepfakes raise serious concerns about privacy, consent, and digital rights, particularly when individuals' likenesses are used without permission, often in harmful or exploitative ways. These issues demand urgent attention from lawmakers, forensic professionals, and civil society to develop robust frameworks that protect individuals while maintaining trust in digital evidence and media integrity.

6.1 Legal and Ethical Implications of Deepfake Technology

Deepfakes and deepfake technology has created a range of legal and ethical challenges that increasingly affect individuals, institutions, and society as a whole. At the heart of these challenges are concerns about privacy, consent, and digital rights. Deepfakes often involve using a real person's face, voice, or likenesses without their permission, exposing individuals to risks such as reputational harm, harassment, and emotional distress.

One of the most critical issues is the rise of non-consensual deepfake pornography, which disproportionately targets women and highlights underlying gendered forms of digital harm. This trend underscores the

 DOI: 10.1201/9781003714811-6

urgent need for stronger legal safeguards to protect personal identity, bodily autonomy, and dignity in online environments.

Beyond violations of privacy and consent, deepfake production frequently depends on existing photographs, videos, and audio recordings to train AI models, raising further concerns around intellectual property and copyright. When synthetic media imitates the likeness of public figures or incorporates copyrighted material (whether branded imagery or creative works) it increasingly blurs the boundary between legitimate transformation and unauthorised use. Enforcement remains complex, as proving ownership, attribution, or malicious intent becomes difficult once deepfakes circulate widely across digital platforms without clear provenance or context.

Deepfakes are increasingly being weaponised for fraud and identity theft, particularly within corporate and financial environments. One high-profile example involved the impersonation of a chief financial officer (CFO) at the multinational firm Arup, where criminals used deepfake video conferencing to deceive an employee into authorising $25 million in wire transfers [1]. Incidents like this highlight the need for multi-layered verification protocols and robust legal safeguards in contexts where trust and identity are fundamental. Similar attacks have targeted energy companies, financial institutions, and public figures, demonstrating that deepfake-enabled fraud is neither isolated nor confined to high-profile individuals.

A further challenge lies in the admissibility and reliability of deepfake evidence in court. Historically, audio and video recordings have been treated as trustworthy forms of proof. However, the rise of sophisticated synthetic media undermines this assumption, as manipulated content can now be almost indistinguishable from authentic footage. Courts must therefore adopt new forensic standards to verify the origin, integrity, and chain of custody of digital evidence. This includes the integration of XAI frameworks, which are essential for ensuring that AI-based assessments (such as the classification of a video as a deepfake) are transparent, reproducible, and legally defensible.

Legislative responses to deepfake misuse remain fragmented and uneven. In the US, some states have introduced targeted laws, such as

California's AB 730 and AB 2655, addressing deceptive political content and non-consensual explicit deepfakes. Yet these measures have faced constitutional challenges. In 2025, for example, a lawsuit backed by X and Elon Musk resulted in the overruling of legislation requiring labels on digitally altered campaign materials, with the court citing federal platform rules and First Amendment concerns. In contrast, the Danish government is pioneering a copyright-based approach to identity protection, proposing amendments that would grant individuals exclusive rights over their facial features, voice, and likeness. If enacted, this would be the first legislation of its kind in Europe, criminalising unauthorised deepfake creation and distribution while preserving key exceptions for parody and satire [2].

Beyond legal concerns, the use of deepfakes raises profound ethical questions surrounding autonomy, dignity, and consent. While deepfakes can have legitimate applications (ranging from education and satire to accessibility tools), the ethical boundary hinges on whether those depicted have provided informed consent. Within law enforcement, deepfake detection is also being used to trace the origins of NCII and CSAM, where fabricated imagery may incorporate the likenesses of real victims. This highlights the need for ethically sound forensic practices and for tools capable of distinguishing between synthetic and real harm, ensuring that investigations do not inadvertently cause further trauma.

6.2 Regulating Synthetic Media: A Global Legal Response

As deepfake and generative AI technologies become more sophisticated and widely accessible, governments around the world are racing to establish legal frameworks that address their potential for harm. From privacy violations and misinformation to electoral interference and non-consensual content, synthetic media poses complex challenges that demand coordinated regulatory action. Recent initiatives such as the UK Online Safety Act 2023, the EU AI Act 2024, the California AI Transparency Act, and the Take It Down Act (both in the United States) illustrate the emerging direction of international law, with the aim of prioritising transparency, accountability, and the protection of individual rights in the digital age.

6.2.1 UK Online Safety Act and the Crime and Policing Bill

The UK's Online Safety Act, which came into force in January 2024, criminalises the sharing of sexually explicit deepfakes and introduces new offences relating to the creation and distribution of intimate images without consent. The subsequent Crime and Policing Bill (2025) expands these provisions by making the creation of deepfakes a standalone criminal offence, carrying a potential prison sentence of up to two years. Together, these laws place significant enforcement responsibilities on platforms and technology providers, with a strong focus on protecting victims (particularly women and girls) from digital abuse. The UK's approach emphasises safeguarding and accountability within online environments. Under the Online Safety Act 2023, platforms are required to proactively identify and remove illegal content, including material related to terrorism, fraud, and sexual abuse. Failure to comply can result in fines of up to 10% of a company's global annual turnover, and senior managers may be held criminally liable if their organisation fails to meet information-request obligations issued by regulators such as Ofcom.

6.2.2 EU AI Act

The EU AI Act, adopted in 2024, is the world's first comprehensive legal framework for artificial intelligence. It classifies AI systems based on risk, with deepfakes falling under the limited-risk category. Article 50 of the Act mandates that synthetic media must be clearly disclosed and detectable. Content creators and platforms are required to label AI-generated content, and non-compliance can result in penalties of up to €35 million or 7% of global turnover. The Act also includes exceptions for artistic and satirical content and encourages the development of sector-specific "Codes of Practice." Its emphasis on transparency and accountability sets a global benchmark for AI regulation.

6.2.3 California AI Transparency Act

The California AI Transparency Act represents a significant step toward regulating generative AI and synthetic media. Effective from

January 2026, the legislation requires AI providers with over one million monthly users to implement transparency measures. These include both manifest disclosures (visible labels) and latent disclosures (embedded metadata) in AI-generated content such as images, videos, and audio. Additionally, platforms and device manufacturers must offer free public AI detection tools and ensure provenance data is accessible. The Act aims to combat deepfake misuse by making synthetic content traceable and verifiable, aligning California's approach with broader international efforts, such as the EU AI Act.

6.2.4 Take It Down Act (US Federal Law)

The Take It Down Act, signed into law in May 2025, is the first federal US legislation specifically targeting non-consensual intimate deepfakes. It criminalises the publication of deepfake and authentic intimate images without consent and mandates that platforms implement a notice-and-takedown system within 48 hours of user notification. Violators face fines and up to three years of imprisonment. This law marks a shift from copyright-based takedown models to personhood-based protections, focusing on consent and harm rather than ownership. It reflects growing recognition of the need to protect individuals from digital impersonation and exploitation.

While the approaches of these various laws can vary – e.g. California and the EU emphasise watermarking and provenance, the UK and US focus on criminal liability and consent – the shared objective is to mitigate harm and uphold trust in digital content. These laws reflect an emerging international consensus: AI-generated media must be traceable, responsibly managed, and subject to legal scrutiny. As deepfake technology continues to evolve, coordinated legal frameworks will be essential to ensure ethical use and protect individuals across borders (Table 6.1). Table 6.1 presents an overview of deepfake regulations and legal remedies.

Table 6.1 Comparative Overview of Deepfake Regulations and Legal Remedies

JURISDICTION	CRIMINAL LAW FRAMEWORKS	CIVIL REMEDIES FOR VICTIMS
United Kingdom	- Malicious Communications Act 1988 - Communications Act 2003 - Fraud Act 2006 - Protection from Harassment Act 1997 - Computer Misuse Act 1990 - Online Safety Act 2023: Section 66B criminalises sharing/threatening to share intimate deepfakes - 2025 amendments: criminalise creation of sexually explicit deepfakes	- Defamation (Defamation Act 2013) - Misuse of private information - Data protection claims (UK GDPR) - Malicious falsehood
European Union	- EU AI Act (2024): Article 50 mandates disclosure of deepfakes - Digital Services Act (DSA) 2022: Article 35 requires labelling of manipulated content - eIDAS 2 Regulation: Enhances digital evidence standards for electronic signatures, timestamps, etc. - National criminal codes vary; some include deepfake-specific offences	- GDPR-based claims for biometric misuse - Civil liability under national tort laws- Image-based abuse laws in some member states - Defamation and privacy actions depending on jurisdiction
United States of America	- Take It Down Act (2025): Criminalises non-consensual intimate deepfakes - NO FAKES Act (Nurture Originals, Foster Art, and Keep Entertainment Safe Act) (proposed): Federal right to control voice/image - FTC Act §5: Targets deceptive deepfake use - Computer Fraud and Abuse Act (CFAA): Criminalises unauthorised access for deepfake creation - State laws: 47 states have deepfake laws (e.g. Texas, California)	- Civil lawsuits for defamation, emotional distress, invasion of privacy - Digital Millennium Copyright Act (DMCA) takedown requests - Federal civil action under VAWA (Violence Against Women Act) (2022) - Right of publicity under the proposed NO FAKES Act

6.2.5 Reporting Deepfakes

Clear and accessible information on how to identify and report suspected deepfakes should be made more widely available to support individuals and practitioners in responding effectively to such harms. When encountering a suspected deepfake, the first step is to confirm and document the evidence. Begin by verifying that the content is indeed a deepfake. Indicators may include unnatural facial movements, mismatched audio, or inconsistent lighting. Once confirmed, gather all relevant details such as URLs, usernames, platform information, and any associated messages. Screenshots or recordings should be taken, along with the date and time of discovery. Also, avoid engaging with the poster – do not comment on or share the content – as this can complicate removal efforts and may lead to the perpetrator blocking you.

The next step is to report the content to the hosting platform. Most major social media services, including Facebook, Instagram, TikTok, X, and YouTube, provide reporting tools for harmful or impersonation content. When submitting a report, select categories such as NCII, impersonation, or harassment. If the platform fails to act promptly, victims may escalate the matter through formal takedown mechanisms, such as the DMCA in the US or GDPR-based requests in the EU.

In cases involving criminal conduct, it is essential to report to law enforcement.

- In the UK, reports can be made via the Police.uk deepfake reporting portal or at a local station. Fraud-related cases should be directed to Action Fraud, while terrorism-related content can be reported through gov.uk/report-terrorism.
- Within the EU, victims should contact national cybercrime units or use Europol channels for cross-border incidents.
- In the US, complaints can be filed with local police or the FBI Internet Crime Complaint Centre (IC3). For non-consensual intimate deepfakes, the Take It Down Act provides a mechanism requiring platforms to remove such content within 48 hours of a valid request.

Victims should also seek legal advice to explore civil remedies. In the UK and EU, these may include actions for defamation, misuse of private information, and GDPR claims. In the US, victims may pursue claims under privacy torts, right of publicity claims, and federal protections such as those provided by the Take It Down Act.

Finally, individuals should take steps to protect themselves from further harm. This includes securing online accounts, enabling strong privacy settings, and monitoring one's digital footprint for misuse. Preventative measures such as watermarking personal images can also help deter manipulation.

If the deepfake involves sexual content, minors, or threats, treat the matter as an emergency. Call 999 in the UK or 911 in the US if there is immediate danger and consider anonymous reporting through services such as Crimestoppers or equivalent hotlines.

6.3 Admissibility and Reliability of Deepfake Evidence in Court

6.3.1 United Kingdom

The admissibility and reliability of deepfake evidence in UK courts is a rapidly evolving legal issue, shaped by technological advances, judicial caution, and emerging statutory frameworks. Admissibility refers to whether a piece of evidence is legally acceptable for consideration in a court of law. For evidence to be admissible, it must typically meet the criteria of relevance, materiality, and competence. This means the evidence must relate directly to the facts of the case, have the potential to influence the outcome, and be obtained and presented in a lawful and procedurally correct manner. Courts also consider whether the evidence is free from undue prejudice, hearsay, or other exclusionary factors that could compromise a fair trial.

Reliability concerns the trustworthiness and accuracy of the evidence presented. It involves evaluating how the evidence was obtained, whether it has been altered or tampered with, and whether it can be independently verified. Reliable evidence is consistent, credible, and derived from a dependable source or method. In the context of digital or AI-generated content, reliability also includes assessing the technical integrity of the data and the validity of any tools or algorithms used to analyse or produce it.

In the UK, the admissibility of digital evidence is governed by principles of relevance, reliability, and fairness under the Police and Criminal Evidence Act 1984 (PACE) and the Criminal Procedure Rules. For digital evidence to be accepted, it must be shown to be authentic, unaltered, and collected in accordance with proper procedures. Courts assess whether the evidence has been tampered with or improperly handled, and whether the chain of custody has been maintained. However, with the rise of AI-generated content such as deepfakes, questions around authenticity and manipulation have become more complex, often requiring expert testimony and technical validation to meet evidentiary standards [3].

UK courts apply general evidentiary principles to deepfake content, including:

- *Relevance*: Evidence must be pertinent to the case.
- *Authenticity*: The proponent must show that the evidence is what it purports to be.
- *Reliability*: Courts assess whether the evidence was produced or altered using trustworthy methods.

However, deepfakes challenge these principles due to their realistic but fabricated nature, making authentication difficult. Judges increasingly rely on expert digital forensic testimony to assess whether digital media has been manipulated. The Crown Prosecution Service (CPS) applies the Code for Crown Prosecutors to determine whether deepfake-related offences meet public interest and evidentiary thresholds. Pre-trial hearings are increasingly used to assess admissibility and reliability.

Jones and Jones address the critical question of how prepared the United Kingdom's justice system is to confront the challenges posed by deepfake audio and video [4]. Their work highlights the vulnerabilities in evidential standards, particularly around authenticity and reproducibility, and emphasises the urgent need for robust forensic methodologies to counter synthetic media. They argues that while legal frameworks and professional practices are evolving, they remain insufficient against the rapid advancement of AI-driven manipulation technologies [3]. Jones advocates for the development of authentication protocols, enhanced training for forensic practitioners, and legislative reforms to safeguard the integrity of judicial processes in an era where digital falsification threatens trust in evidence and due process.

Sandoval et al. conducted a comprehensive review of how deepfakes threaten the integrity of criminal justice systems worldwide [5]. It identifies key risks, including the erosion of trust in digital evidence, the potential for fabricated media to influence investigations and trials, and the emergence of "plausible deniability," where genuine evidence can be dismissed as fake [4]. The review categorises deepfake-related crimes such as fraud, identity theft, sexual exploitation, and political misinformation, highlighting their growing prevalence. It also examines current detection technologies and legal frameworks, noting significant gaps in standardisation, explainability, and cross-border enforcement. The authors call for multi-stakeholder collaboration, improved forensic methodologies, and legislative reforms to safeguard judicial processes against synthetic media manipulation.

6.3.2 European Union

The admissibility and reliability of deepfake evidence in EU courts is shaped by traditional evidentiary principles and emerging regulatory frameworks under the EU AI Act 2024, Digital Services Act (DSA) 2022, and national laws. Evidence must meet criteria of relevance, authenticity, and lawfulness, while respecting fundamental rights under the Charter of Fundamental Rights of the EU and GDPR. Courts also weigh whether admitting such evidence could cause undue prejudice or infringe privacy rights.

Reliability involves assessing the technical integrity of the data, the robustness of detection tools, and the transparency of algorithms used to create or analyse the material. However, deepfakes present unique challenges: their hyper-realistic nature makes manipulation difficult to detect, and the black-box architecture of many AI systems complicates judicial scrutiny and cross-examination.

Under the EU AI Act (Regulation (EU) 2024/1689), systems generating synthetic media such as deepfakes fall under limited-risk AI and are subject to transparency obligations. Article 50 requires providers and deployers of generative AI systems to ensure outputs are marked in a machine-readable format and detectable as artificially generated or manipulated. Deployers must disclose when content constitutes a deepfake, unless exempt for artistic or law enforcement purposes. These obligations aim to prevent deception and support evidentiary integrity, but they do not automatically guarantee admissibility in court. Judges must still evaluate whether the evidence meets procedural and substantive standards, often relying on expert testimony to explain detection methods and limitations.

The DSA complements these requirements by imposing duties on very large online platforms to label manipulated content and mitigate systemic misinformation risks. While primarily aimed at platform governance, these provisions indirectly support evidentiary reliability by promoting traceability and accountability.

Judicial practice remains fragmented across Member States. Some apply existing criminal provisions, such as Germany's §201a StGB (Strafgesetzbuch – German Criminal Code) on violations of personal rights, while others rely on general offences like harassment, fraud, or defamation. Expert reviews and advanced digital forensic AI tools are recommended, but studies highlight their current limitations and bias risks, reinforcing the need for human oversight and standardized protocols. Bench cards and pre-trial hearings are advocated to address questions of source, chain of custody, and alterations, alongside mandatory disclosure of AI involvement.

6.3.3 United States

In the US, digital evidence must comply with the Federal Rules of Evidence (FRE), particularly:

- *Rule 401 (Relevance):* Evidence must be relevant to the facts in dispute.
- *Rule 901 (Authentication):* The proponent must demonstrate that the evidence is what it claims to be.
- *Rule 702 (Expert Testimony):* Expert opinions must be based on reliable principles and methods.

Courts evaluating technical or scientific evidence often apply the Daubert standard, which assesses the reliability and validity of the methodology used. Under this standard, judges consider whether the method has been empirically tested, whether it has undergone peer review, its known or potential error rate, and whether it is generally accepted within the relevant scientific community [6].

This standard is critical when assessing outputs from deepfake detectors and/or AI-based forensic tools, such as deepfake detection systems. Courts require that the processes used to generate or analyse digital evidence are scientifically valid and transparent. However, the black-box nature of many AI systems poses challenges for transparency and cross-examination, potentially undermining the credibility of such evidence in court. As a result, jurisdictions are responding to the need to update legal frameworks to accommodate the complexities introduced by synthetic and deepfake media, and AI-driven analysis [7].

FRE 707 is a proposed federal evidence rule that ensures AI-generated evidence is subjected to the same reliability requirements as expert testimony under the Daubert standard [8]. When machine-generated evidence is offered without a human expert, judges must still evaluate it using the reliability criteria of Rule 702. Under FRE 707:

- Machine-generated evidence may only be admitted if it satisfies the requirements of Rule 702(a)–(d). These include demonstrating that the method is reliable, based on sufficient data, and applied reliably to the case at hand.
- If an AI output would normally require an expert to introduce it, the proponent must establish scientific reliability even if no human expert explains the process.

To mitigate risks associated with suspected AI-generated evidence, judges (and other legal professionals) are encouraged to adopt structured practices that promote transparency and reliability. This includes using bench cards and checklists to ensure consistency, asking targeted questions about the source of the evidence, the integrity of the chain of custody, and any alterations or manipulations that may have occurred. Additionally, courts should require expert testimony to explain the detection methods used and their limitations. These measures help ensure that AI-generated evidence is scrutinised under the same rigorous standards applied to traditional forensic evidence, safeguarding fairness and due process.

6.4 Explainability and the Legal Use of AI in Deepfake Detection

As AI models become increasingly integrated into digital forensic workflows, particularly for detecting deepfakes, the issue of explainability has emerged as a central concern in legal contexts. Explainability refers to the ability of an AI system to make its decision-making process understandable and interpretable to humans. This is essential when AI-generated conclusions are presented as evidence in court, where transparency, reproducibility, and accountability are long-established legal standards.

6.4.1 Legal Standards of Evidence

Courts require that all forms of digital evidence meet rigorous criteria: it must be transparent, reproducible, and capable of being independently verified. As identified, many AI models (especially deep learning systems) do not explain how they reached a particular conclusion. For example, when an AI tool labels a video as a deepfake, it must be able to justify that determination in terms that legal professionals and juries can understand. Without such clarity, the evidentiary value of such outputs is significantly weakened and may not meet admissibility thresholds.

6.4.2 Cross-Examination and Expert Testimony

In courtroom settings, forensic experts must be prepared to defend the outputs of AI-based tools under cross-examination. If a model's underlying logic is opaque or proprietary, this not only undermines the credibility of the evidence but also the expert who presents it. Courts may reject AI-generated findings if their reasoning cannot be articulated in a legally sound and scientifically defensible way.

For this reason, expert testimony involving AI-assisted analysis must rely on transparent, reproducible methodologies that allow legal decision-makers to evaluate how conclusions were reached. To support this, vendors should be obligated to provide comprehensive technical documentation (such as model cards, validated use-cases, and reproducibility reports) tailored for courtroom scrutiny. Building a network of trained expert witnesses and standardised testimony frameworks for synthetic media would further enhance consistency and credibility across legal proceedings.

6.4.3 Due Process and Fair Trial

Defendants have a fundamental right to challenge the evidence presented against them. If an AI system's reasoning cannot be explained or interrogated, it risks violating principles of procedural fairness and due process. This is particularly problematic in cases involving manipulated media, where the defence must be able to question not only the conclusion but the method by which that conclusion was reached. The use of opaque AI systems therefore raises significant ethical and legal concerns for justice systems reliant on transparency.

6.4.4 Technical Challenges to Explainable AI (XAI)

Despite its importance, implementing XAI in forensic contexts remains technically challenging:

- *Model complexity:* Deep learning models, such as neural networks with millions of parameters, are inherently difficult to interpret. Different models may produce varying results for the same input, raising questions about reliability and consistency.
- *Lack of standardised outputs:* Many detection tools offer binary results (e.g. "real" or "fake") without confidence scores or feature-level explanations. Some tools may detect AI-generated images but fail to identify manipulations like face-swapping between real images, leading to incomplete assessments.
- *Proprietary systems:* Commercial forensic tools often operate as closed systems, withholding details about their internal algorithms. This lack of transparency further limits their admissibility and trustworthiness in court.

Without robust XAI frameworks, integrating AI into forensic practice risks undermining the very evidentiary standards it is intended to support. Ensuring that AI-generated evidence is legally admissible and ethically sound will require sustained collaboration between developers, forensic practitioners, legal professionals, and policymakers. Ultimately, AI systems used in deepfake detection must be not only accurate but also explainable, auditable, and defensible.

6.5 Key Risks and Policy Recommendations

Deepfake technology is no longer merely a technical problem; it represents a systemic threat to justice, democratic integrity, and fundamental human rights. Policymakers must act urgently to establish robust legal standards, enforce ethical safeguards, and ensure technological accountability to maintain public trust in digital evidence and protect individuals from escalating forms of harm.

The following section sets out key legal and actionable policy recommendations to guide this response.

6.5.1 Key Risks

- *Evidentiary integrity*: Deepfakes undermine authenticity and reliability standards in courts, creating "plausible deniability" where genuine evidence can be dismissed as fake. This erosion of trust in media destabilises long-standing evidentiary standards and places greater pressure on courts to adopt new forensic verification methods.
- *Privacy violations*: Non-consensual intimate deepfakes, identity cloning, and the misuse of facial likenesses inflict profound emotional, reputational, and sometimes professional harm. Victims (disproportionately women and minors) often face harassment, blackmail, and a loss of control over their personal identity. The permanence and viral spread of synthetic content compound these harms, making legal recourse difficult and recovery incomplete.
- *Fraud and misinformation*: Synthetic media is increasingly weaponised for financial scams, social engineering attacks, political manipulation, and targeted harassment. High-fidelity audio and video impersonations have enabled multi-million-dollar corporate fraud, while deepfakes of public figures are used to distort public discourse, influence elections, and undermine trust in democratic institutions. These threats scale rapidly as generative AI tools become cheaper and more accessible.
- *Technological opacity*: Many AI detection and generation systems function as "black boxes," offering limited insight into how conclusions are reached. This opacity complicates expert testimony, weakens the defensibility of AI-generated findings, and challenges due process rights. Without explainable, auditable systems, courts struggle to scrutinise AI outputs, and forensic experts face credibility risks when cross-examined on proprietary or non-transparent methods.

Policy Recommendations

1. Mandate Provenance and Labelling of AI-Generated Media

Requirements

- Developers and major platforms must attach tamper-evident provenance metadata (content credentials) or visible labels to AI-generated or AI-altered images, audio, and video at creation or upload.

- Use standards-based formats (e.g. Coalition for Content Provenance and Authenticity (C2PA) content credentials) for interoperability and trust.

Rationale
Provenance enables tracing origin and editing history, improving trust, supporting triage by platforms and courts, and reducing misinformation risks.

Implementation

- Incentivise adoption via regulatory requirements for large platforms and major AI-model providers.
- Provide phased compliance timelines and technical guidance.
- Include editor and toolchain metadata, ideally signed by originators.
- Allow opt-outs for clearly marked parody/satire with explicit flags.
- Combine technical measures (e.g. watermarking, machine-readable labels) with global regulatory frameworks similar to the EU Digital Services Act.

2. Transparency from AI Model Providers

Requirements
AI model providers (particularly large-model hosts) must:

- Implement technical measures to enable downstream attribution, including robust, hard-to-remove watermarks or cryptographic signatures for model outputs.
- Maintain auditable logs of model outputs and high-risk usage to support accountability and investigations.

Rationale
Watermarking and provenance tied to models help detect synthetic content, attribute misuse, and deter malicious re-use.

Implementation

- Develop standards for watermark robustness and public test suites.
- Require proportionate logging for high-risk scenarios (e.g. identity impersonation).
- Ensure access to logs follows legal due process.

3. Labelling and Expedited Takedown

Requirements

- Platforms must clearly label suspected AI-generated content.
- Implement expedited removal pathways for illicit material (e.g. non-consensual intimate deepfakes) with transparent appeals and safeguards.

Rationale
Manipulated media can spread rapidly and cause immediate harm. Combining prompt platform action with clear labelling reduces both reach and user confusion.

Implementation
Removal triggers should be narrowly defined, for example:

- Verified complaints of non-consensual intimate content
- Credible legal orders

Platforms should also publish regular transparency reports detailing takedowns, appeals, and enforcement actions. When they follow established notice-and-action procedures, they should receive safe harbour protections, meaning legal immunity from liability for user-generated content. To retain this protection, a platform must operate as a "*mere conduit*" or "*neutral host,*" avoiding excessive editorial control over the content it carries. Once a platform steps outside this neutral role, it may become legally responsible for unlawful material on its services. Safe harbour is lost under two key circumstances:

- *Actual Knowledge:* The platform becomes aware of illegal content or activity and fails to act promptly to remove or disable access to it.
- *Active Participation*: The platform plays a substantive role in creating, shaping, or developing the illegal content, rather than simply hosting it.

4. Protecting Victims and Establishing Civil and Criminal Remedies

Requirements
Laws should guarantee accessible, timely, and effective remedies for individuals harmed by malicious deepfakes (including NCII, identity

misuse, fraud, impersonation, harassment, and reputational damage). Effective remedies must include rapid takedown procedures, appropriate civil damages, expedited injunctive relief, and criminal penalties for intentional or aggravated offences. Victim-support mechanisms, including counselling services and access to legal assistance, should be made available as a statutory right.

Rationale

Deepfake harms are often immediate, severe, and difficult to reverse due to the viral spread and persistent replication of synthetic media. Victims require swift and meaningful remedies to prevent ongoing harm, restore their autonomy, and hold offenders accountable. Traditional legal processes are often too slow, too costly, or unsuited to the unique challenges of AI-generated media. Clear legal remedies ensure consistency across cases and strengthen deterrence.

Implementation

- Establish rapid takedown and emergency response mechanisms, requiring platforms to remove harmful deepfakes within defined timeframes (e.g. 48 hours) upon validated notice.
- Create expedited judicial pathways for emergency injunctions, enabling courts to issue takedown orders, preservation requests, or restraint of distribution at short notice.
- Define harm-based civil remedies, including statutory damages, compensation for reputational and psychological harm, and recovery of financial losses in fraud cases.
- Introduce proportionate criminal penalties that escalate depending on intent, scale, and impact: ranging from fines and restraining orders to custodial sentences for severe or repeat offences.
- Mandate platform cooperation, including secure evidence preservation (e.g. logs, metadata) to support investigations and legal proceedings.
- Provide dedicated victim support services, (such as counselling, legal support) on digital hygiene and evidence collection, ensuring victims are informed and supported throughout the process.

5. Support public education and sector playbooks

Requirements
Governments and regulators should fund national awareness campaigns, media literacy programmes, and sector-specific response playbooks tailored to high-risk domains such as finance, the judiciary, healthcare, and elections. These resources must provide practical guidance on identifying, reporting, and mitigating synthetic media threats.

Rationale
Technical and legal measures alone cannot counter the speed and scale at which deepfakes and AI-generated misinformation spread. Public resilience is a critical layer of defence: individuals, organisations, and frontline professionals must be equipped to recognise manipulated content, understand its risks, and take appropriate action. Without a baseline level of public and institutional literacy, even the strongest regulatory framework will have limited impact.

Implementation

- Develop and fund cross-sector training programmes including workshops, simulation exercises, and scenario-based activities for corporations, law enforcement, the judiciary (and other legal professionals), and public agencies.
- Produce sector-specific playbooks covering risk indicators, verification steps, escalation protocols, and recommended tools. For high-risk areas (e.g. courts, insurance, elections), provide standardised templates such as incident-response forms, reporting checklists, and chain-of-custody documentation for suspected deepfake evidence.
- Coordinate public education efforts with national media outlets, schools, universities, and private-sector partners to promote responsible content verification and critical engagement with digital media.
- Integrate deepfake awareness into existing cyber hygiene and misinformation resilience programmes, ensuring that guidance reaches vulnerable groups as well as professionals in critical roles.

6. Promote international cooperation and common technical standards
International cooperation is essential for addressing the cross-border nature of synthetic media threats. Governments should support the

development of technical standards and coordinated enforcement mechanisms that enable effective action against deepfake misuse, recognising that these harms routinely transcend national jurisdictions. This includes working with global initiatives (e.g. United Nations and Interpol) and aligning technical and legal standards for content labelling, provenance tracking, evidentiary handling, and cross-border takedown procedures. Harmonising criminal definitions and investigative protocols will further strengthen the global response to transnational deepfake-related offences.

In parallel, jurisdictions should enhance both criminal and civil remedies to better protect victims and deter misuse. Legal frameworks must be aligned to ensure consistent treatment of deepfake-related harms, while expanding victim protections to cover privacy violations, reputational damage, and other forms of digitally facilitated abuse.

7. Building Forensic and Legal Capability

Alongside technological development, implement training programs for judges, lawyers, and law enforcement to build expertise in handling AI-generated evidence. Additionally, development of reference use-cases, best practices, and practical "*what to do*" guides to educate legal professionals and affected sectors on managing deepfake-related risks effectively will improve overall capabilities.

Sample Checklist for Organisations

Risk Prevention

- ☐ Require disclosure for synthetic media in advertising, training, and communication
- ☐ Implement content-credential systems for internal media production
- ☐ Introduce multi-factor verification for sensitive video, audio, and identity workflows
- ☐ Train staff to recognise deepfake red flags

Response to Suspected Deepfakes

- ☐ Stop distribution of suspicious media immediately
- ☐ Preserve original content and notify security or compliance teams
- ☐ Validate identity through known channels before acting on requests

- ☐ Engage digital forensics experts when manipulation would affect financial or reputational decisions

Governance and Policy

- ☐ Maintain an internal AI-media disclosure policy
- ☐ Require third-party vendors to declare synthetic media use
- ☐ Conduct annual reviews of detection tools and protocols
- ☐ Ensure privacy-protecting practices when storing provenance or metadata

Sample Checklist for Legal Professionals

Before Admitting Digital Evidence

- ☐ Has the submitting party declared any AI involvement in generating or altering the material?
- ☐ Is metadata preserved and unaltered (format, encoding history, timestamps)?
- ☐ Was a hash generated at the point of acquisition?
- ☐ Is provenance data (watermark, signature, content credentials) included?

During Evaluation

- ☐ Has a certified examiner assessed authenticity?
- ☐ Does the report include method, error rates, confidence intervals, and tool limitations?
- ☐ Are there contextual inconsistencies or manipulation indicators?
- ☐ Are detection tools scientifically validated and admissible under jurisdictional standards?

Before Ruling

- ☐ Is uncertainty clearly communicated and accounted for?
- ☐ Are alternative explanations or corroborating evidence considered?
- ☐ Does the chain of custody contain any gaps?

Sample Checklist for Investigators

Initial Handling

- Preserve original files without conversion or compression
- Secure device or source and document acquisition process

- Generate cryptographic hashes
- Record context: who submitted the file, how, and when

Authentication Process

- Extract and examine metadata (including signs of re-encoding)
- Conduct preliminary screening using approved tools
- Identify visual/audio red flags (e.g. lighting, boundary artefacts)
- Forward to certified audio/video analysts if complex manipulation is suspected

Documentation and Reporting

- Maintain a complete chain of custody
- Record all analysis methods and tools used
- Note limitations and uncertainty levels
- Store original and analysed files in secure systems

6.6 Summary

The rapid evolution of deepfake technology presents a complex landscape of legal, ethical, and evidentiary challenges across the globe. While regulatory frameworks are beginning to address the misuse of synthetic media, significant gaps remain in enforcement, cross-jurisdictional coordination, and public awareness. The process of reporting deepfakes must be strengthened through clearer legal definitions, streamlined mechanisms for victims and investigators, and enhanced collaboration between platforms, law enforcement, and forensic experts. Crucially, the admissibility and reliability of deepfake evidence in court hinge on the development of robust forensic standards, transparent AI tools, and explainable methodologies that align with legal principles of fairness and due process. As deepfake technology continues to advance, it is imperative that legal systems evolve in parallel, ensuring that justice is not compromised by technological opacity, and that forensic evidence remains credible and accountable.

References

[1] Adaptive Security, 'Arup's $25M deepfake loss: Anatomy of an AI-powered scam', Available: www.adaptivesecurity.com/blog/arup-deepfake-scam-attack.

[2] S. Karttunen, 'At a glance The Danish approach to copyright and deepfakes: A model for the EU?', EU, Jan. 2026. Available: https://eprs.in.ep.europa.eu/

[3] A. Bhattathiri, F. Sharma, and A. Purohit, 'Deepfake in the courtroom: Legal challenges and evidentiary standards', in *Digital Doppelgangers: The Rise of Deepfakes & Artificial Intelligence*, India: Lex Assisto, 2025. Available: www.researchgate.net/publication/390200521

[4] K. O. Jones and B. S. Jones, 'How robust is the United Kingdom justice system against the advance of deepfake audio and video?', in *Proceedings of the 36th International Conference on Information Technologies (InfoTech-2022)*, Bulgaria: IEEE, Sep. 2022, pp. 13–24.

[5] M. P. Sandoval, M. de Almeida Vau, J. Solaas, and L. Rodrigues, 'Threat of deepfakes to the criminal justice system: A systematic review', Dec. 01, 2024, BioMed Central Ltd. doi: 10.1186/s40163-024-00239-1.

[6] J. Robinson, 'Daubert Standard', Legal Information Institute. Cornell Law School. Available: www.law.cornell.edu/wex/daubert_standard.

[7] F. Romero-Moreno, 'Deepfake detection in generative AI: A legal framework proposal to protect human rights', *Computer Law & Security Review*, vol. 58, p. 106162, Sep. 2025, doi: 10.1016/j.clsr.2025.106162.

[8] Practical Law Litigation, 'Proposed FRE 707 and AI evidence in Federal Court', Thomson Reuters Practical Law. https://uk.practicallaw.thomsonreuters.com/w-047-4475?transitionType=Default&contextData=(sc.Default)&firstPage=true.

7

Combating the Deepfake Threat

Tools and Strategies

As deepfake and fabricated media technologies continue to evolve in sophistication and accessibility, the urgency to develop robust countermeasures has intensified across sectors. This chapter explores the emerging landscape of technologies designed to detect and authenticate deepfakes, highlighting cutting-edge approaches rooted in AI, biometrics, and multimedia forensics. It also examines industry-recommended tools and frameworks currently deployed to mitigate the risks posed by synthetic media, offering practical insights into their capabilities, limitations, and adoption across professional domains. By bridging technological innovation with real-world application, the chapter aims to inform researchers, technologists, and decision-makers navigating the complex terrain of media authenticity in the age of AI.

7.1 Emerging Technologies for Deepfake Detection and Authentication

Today's forensic tools show promise in detecting synthetic media, but they remain inconsistent and often unreliable in operational settings. As previously noted, a study by Australia's CSIRO, in collaboration with Sungkyunkwan University, assessed 16 leading deepfake detectors and found that none could consistently identify deepfakes in real-world scenarios [1]. Many tools produced false positives, false negatives, or ambiguous probability scores that resulted in "undetermined" or "uncertain" classifications [2, 3]. Table 7.1 summarises the types of errors and outcomes commonly encountered in deepfake detection tools.

DOI: 10.1201/9781003714811-7

These limitations pose significant challenges for forensic practice, where clarity, reproducibility, and evidentiary integrity are essential. The same piece of media can produce different outcomes depending on the tool, model version, or system configuration used. Even when a detector concludes that a video is not AI-generated, the content may still have been manipulated through traditional editing techniques, e.g. frame-by-frame editing, splicing, face swapping with non-AI images (that fall outside the scope of many AI-focused classifiers).

Detection accuracy is further affected by a range of contextual factors, including media quality, compression level, lighting, editing artefacts, and the specific manipulation type. Many deepfake detectors and AI–based detectors often produce inconsistent results across repeated tests, reflecting broader issues in machine learning systems where model stability and generalisability remain ongoing challenges.

Table 7.1 Deepfake Detection Outcomes and Error Types

OUTCOME TYPE	DEFINITION	IMPLICATIONS IN FORENSIC CONTEXT
True Positive (TP)	The system correctly identifies a deepfake as synthetic	Supports investigative accuracy and strengthens evidential claims.
True Negative (TN)	The system correctly identified authentic media as genuine	Confirms media integrity. Useful for ruling out manipulation
False Positive (FP)	The system incorrectly flags genuine media as a deepfake	Risks undermining trust in authentic evidence May lead to wrongful suspicion or dismissal of valid content
False Negative (FN)	The system fails to detect a deepfake, classifying it as authentic	Allows manipulated content to pass as genuine Poses serious risks in legal, journalistic, or security settings
Uncertain/Undetermined	The system cannot confidently classify the media; outputs a probability or an ambiguous result	Creates ambiguity. Complicates decision-making and evidential reporting (especially in court or policy settings)

For police DFUs and investigative workflows, the challenge of deepfake detection is compounded by the need for industry-approved tools that meet legal, procedural, and evidential standards. While many open-source solutions demonstrate technical sophistication, they often cannot be adopted in operational settings due to concerns around validation, reproducibility, and admissibility in court. This creates a critical gap in the availability of robust forensic technologies capable of reliably handling synthetic media in real-world investigations.

In response to these limitations, multimedia forensic procedures have emerged as essential components of deepfake detection and authentication. These approaches combine technical analysis with investigative methodologies to verify the integrity and origin of digital content [4]. Deepfake forensics does not focus solely on deepfake detection; it is a comprehensive discipline that integrates multiple layers of analysis, such as:

- *Format and metadata inspection:* inconsistencies or tampering in EXIF data, file structures, or container formats.
- *Scene and physics analysis:* impossible reflections, strange limb positions, or inconsistent motion dynamics.
- *Contextual investigation:* who created the content, when and where it was posted, and how it spread.
- *Signal-based forensic tools:* compression artefacts, inconsistencies in lighting, shadows, focus, sensor noise, or encoding.
- *AI-based detection:* inconsistencies typical of known deepfake generation methods, e.g. irregular pixel-level noise, unnatural blending, or mismatched lighting and shadows.

7.1.1 Methods and Approaches

Multimedia forensic authentication encompasses a suite of scientific techniques used to verify the integrity, origin, and authenticity of digital media – including images, videos, and audio files. These methods are critical in identifying manipulated content, establishing provenance, and supporting efforts in legal investigations, journalism, cybersecurity, and public trust in digital information [5]. With the rise of AI-generated synthetic media, particularly deepfakes, the field has expanded to include advanced detection strategies that address the unique challenges posed by hyper-realistic forgeries. The principal categories of forensic authentication now include passive (blind) techniques, active methods, AI-based detection, and provenance verification [6].

7.1.1.1 Passive (Blind) Forensic Techniques

Passive techniques operate without any prior knowledge of the media's origin or embedded markers. They rely on intrinsic characteristics of the media itself to detect signs of manipulation. These methods are especially valuable for analysing content already in circulation, including deepfakes. Key techniques include metadata examination, hexadecimal analysis, manipulation detection, and examining file integrity which are outlined as follows.

7.1.1.1.1 Metadata Examination

Metadata examination is a vital component of digital forensic investigations because it reveals hidden information embedded within files, offering insights into their origin, history, and potential tampering. By analysing metadata, investigators can determine when, how, and by whom a file was created or modified, making it an essential tool for verifying authenticity. This process often involves examining EXIF data in images and header information in video or audio files to detect anomalies in timestamps, device identifiers, or editing software records. Importantly, metadata analysis is not only about what is present but also what is missing. Authentic images typically include details such as camera model, exposure settings, GPS coordinates, and device IDs. By contrast, AI-generated or -manipulated media may lack these markers or contain fabricated metadata designed to mislead investigators.

What to Analyse

Timestamps

- *Modification Date*: Indicates edits or changes.
- *Access Date*: Shows when the file was last opened.
- *Creation Date*: When the file was originally generated.

Item of interest: A creation date that is later than the modification date or inconsistent with other evidence.

Device information: Camera make and model, operating system, and software used.

Items of interest: Metadata showing editing software (e.g. Adobe Photoshop) when the file is claimed to be original. EXIF or device metadata indicating a different camera model or manufacturer than the one claimed or expected. Tags showing that the file originated from an unexpected OS or device (e.g. mobile metadata in a file claimed to come from a CCTV system).

Editing history: Information showing whether a file has been modified, re-encoded, compressed, or passed through editing or social media processing pipelines.

Item of interest: Metadata stripped or altered, which often happens when files are processed through social media platforms or editing tools.

Other signs of manipulation include:

- Missing or inconsistent metadata fields
- GPS coordinates that do not match the claimed location
- Presence of tags from image/video editing software
- Variation in noise patterns, lighting consistency, or compression artefacts that may point to tampering
- Timestamps that conflict with known timelines

1	Filename	Black Cat Coffee.png	
2	Full Path	C:\Users\	
3	MD5	174dd97a7799b01f7a4a539b91e1	
4	Decoded Pixels MD5	6fcede1fbf8385cae289edbcc747	
5	Format	PNG	Format is not a standard one
6	Format Description	Portable Network Graphics	
7	Image Encoded Size	1024 x 1536	
8	Image Displayed Size	1024 x 1536	
9	Image Normalized Size	1536 x 1024	
10	Aspect Ratio	1.50	
11	Number of Channels	3	
12	BPP	24	
13	Thumbnail Size		Thumbnail is missing
14	Thumbnail Normalized Size		
15	Preview Size		
16	Preview Normalized Size		
17	Exif rotate tag		
18	Number of Exif fields	0	
19	Number of MakerNotes fields	0	
20	Number of IPTC fields	0	
21	Number of XMP fields	0	
22	Number of Photoshop fields	0	
23	Number of ICC fields	0	
24	Exif Make		EXIF Make is missing
25	Exif Model		EXIF Model is missing

Figure 7.1 Deepfake sample EXIF data using Amped Authenticate.

For example, Figure 7.1 shows an example of a file with EXIF data and format size that has been identified as suspicious.

Understanding editing history is essential for assessing authenticity and identifying whether a file has been manipulated (even if AI detection tools classify it as "not AI-generated"). It supports accurate reconstruction of the file's lifecycle and aids in validating or challenging claims about its originality.

7.1.1.1.2 Hexadecimal Analysis

Hexadecimal analysis is the process of examining a file's or disk's raw binary data using a hexadecimal editor to uncover hidden, deleted, or altered information [7]. It allows investigators to see data in its native format, which is essential for finding evidence like fragments of deleted files, malicious code, or hidden messages that are not visible in a standard file view.

Viewing Raw Data

Investigators use hex editors to view the raw, one-dimensional binary data that makes up a file or an entire disk. This data is presented as a sequence of hexadecimal numbers, often alongside the corresponding text characters. For example, JPEG/JFIF is the most common format for storing and transmitting photographic images on the Internet. JPEG files (compressed images) start with an image marker which always contains the marker code hex values "FF D8 FF" – as seen in Figure 7.2 and Table 7.2.

```
0x00000000: FF D8 FF E0  00 10 4A 46  49 46 00 01  01 00 00 01   ......JFIF......
0x00000010: 00 01 00 00  FF DB 00 43  00 06 04 05  06 05 04 06   .......C........
0x00000020: 06 05 06 07  07 06 08 0A  10 0A 0A 09  09 0A 14 0E   ................
0x00000030: 0F 0C 10 17  14 18 18 17  14 16 16 1A  1D 25 1F 1A   .............%..
0x00000040: 1B 23 1C 16  16 20 2C 20  23 26 27 29  2A 29 19 1F   .#... , #&')*)..
0x00000050: 2D 30 2D 28  30 25 28 29  28 FF DB 00  43 01 07 07   -0-(0%()(...C...
0x00000060: 07 0A 08 0A  13 0A 0A 13  28 1A 16 1A  28 28 28 28   ........(...((((
0x00000070: 28 28 28 28  28 28 28 28  28 28 28 28  28 28 28 28   ((((((((((((((((
```

Figure 7.2 JPEG Hexadecimal values.

Table 7.2 File Format Indicators

FORMAT	IDENTIFYING HEX	EDITABLE REGIONS	EDUCATIONAL NOTES
JPEG	Starts with FF D8 FF (SOI marker) APP segments: FF E0 (JFIF), FF E1 (EXIF), FF ED (Photoshop)	EXIF, XMP, IPTC, quantisation tables	Camera images contain rich EXIF; edited or AI-generated images often lack or alter these fields
PNG	Always begins with 89 50 4E 47 0D 0A 1A 0A	tEXt/iTXt chunks for "Software"	Many editors add a "Software" chunk
TIFF	II or MM byte order header Tag 34377 (Photoshop)	TIFF tags incl. XMP/ EXIF	Editors often preserve TIFF tags differently
PSD	Starts with 38 42 50 53	Internal layer structure	Native Photoshop only
RIFF (AVI/ WAV)	Starts with 52 49 46 46	Header chunks (e.g. LIST, INFO)	Used in audio/video; editing software often leaves traces in INFO chunks

We should note that images generated by ChatGPT/DALL·E are standard PNG or JPEG files. They do not contain any special byte pattern, header value, or hex signature that uniquely identifies them as OpenAI-generated.

The file header looks like any normal PNG or JPEG header:

- *PNG starts with:* 89 50 4E 47 0D 0A 1A 0A
- *JPEG starts with:* FF D8 FF

While hex signatures are not present, you *might* find clues in metadata (if the platform includes them). Some AI tools embed metadata such as "Software tag," e.g. "Software: DALLE," "Software: Midjourney," "Software: Stable Diffusion."

AI-generated XMP tags (sometimes) embed data, e.g. XMP:ImageGenerator XMP:AI Model, or proprietary identifiers (which can sometimes be removed).

7.1.1.1.3 Examining File Integrity

Hexadecimal analysis can be used to verify the integrity of evidence by comparing the hex dump of a file against a known good copy or a hash value to detect unauthorised changes or tampering (Figure 7.3).

Id	Name	Evidence Image Value
1	Result:	Image is compatible with Social Media Platform signature(s) in the DB
2	Compatible Social Media Platform(s):	Twitter, Tumblr
3	Classification Source:	Internal database, Internal database
4	Closest File Id:	44db346f364b66d26fb713ea024d0119, a4f8c44f1ec1de0de082f6390feb1ebb
5	Optional message:	Filename does not match any known Tumblr naming scheme

Figure 7.3 File integrity example.

Also, altering specific hex values can hide data or change how an image is displayed. For example, modifying the hex values for an image's height or width can crop an image without deleting the underlying data (which can still be recovered forensically) (Figure 7.4).

5	Format	PNG	Format is not a standard one
6	Format Description	Portable Network Graphics	
7	Image Encoded Size	235 x 287	Resolution is low (235 < 640 Odd width (235 is not multip Odd height (287 is not multi
8	Image Displayed Size	235 x 287	
9	Image Normalized Size	287 x 235	
10	Aspect Ratio	1.22	Odd aspect ratio
11	Number of Channels	4	Channels count different fro
12	BPP	32	BPP (32 different 24)
13	Thumbnail Size		Thumbnail is missing
14	Thumbnail Normalized Size		
15	Preview Size		
16	Preview Normalized Size		
17	Exif rotate tag		
18	Number of Exif fields	0	
19	Number of MakerNotes fields	0	
20	Number of IPTC fields	0	
21	Number of XMP fields	0	
22	Number of Photoshop fields	0	
23	Number of ICC fields	0	
24	Exif Make		EXIF Make is missing
25	Exif Model		EXIF Model is missing
26	Exif Software		

Figure 7.4 Further example of EXIF data.

Other helpful analyses include understanding the low-level structure of a file, which can be essential for data recovery or investigation when file system information is damaged; performing pixel-level analysis to identify inconsistencies in lighting, shadows, reflections, or geometry that may indicate compositing or tampering; examining noise patterns, since each camera sensor produces a unique noise signature whose disruption can reveal altered or spliced regions; and detecting compression artefacts through techniques such as error level analysis (ELA), which highlights areas with differing compression levels that often signal editing.

Figure 7.5 is an AI-generated image of "a black cat drinking coffee" using M365 Copilot, built on the GPT-5 chat model.

Figure 7.5 AI-generated image of a cat drinking coffee created by GPT 5.0. Created using ChatGPT-5 following a prompt to: generate an image of a black cat drinking coffee. AI Tool Attribution: Image generated using M365 Copilot (GPT-5).

This image was then edited in MS Paint using its AI-powered edit tool to remove the handle of the mug. It is used here to demonstrate how compression artefacts can be detected through techniques such as ELA, which highlights areas with differing compression levels that often indicate editing. FotoForensics, the tool of choice for this demonstration, is an online digital image-forensics platform designed to identify signs of manipulation in photos [8]. Note the area where the mug's handle originally was, as shown in Figure 7.6. Similarly, Amped Authenticate ADJPEG (aligned double JPEG) has an updated feature that highlights compression history and area of change in JPEG images, specifically when the 8x8 pixel blocks are aligned.

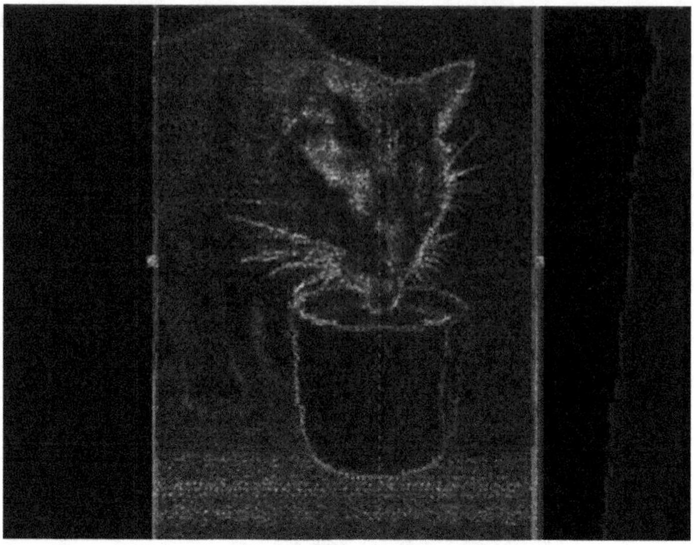

Figure 7.6 Error level analysis of cat drinking coffee.

The visible outline around the cup suggests varying compression levels, which is a common artefact of image editing. When the handle was removed, the altered region was recompressed differently than the original image, creating inconsistencies in JPEG quantisation and block patterns. These differences often manifest as edge halos or abrupt transitions in compression quality. Such anomalies can be detected using forensic techniques like ELA and colour filter array (CFA) analysis, which identifies inconsistencies in the de-mosaicking process used by digital cameras, and is useful for detecting tampered regions.

7.1.1.2 Active Forensic Techniques

Active methods involve embedding information into media at the time of creation or using controlled environments to facilitate later verification. These techniques offer strong guarantees of authenticity but are limited by their dependence on specialised tools and prior setup.

Examples of active forensic techniques include:

- *Digital watermarking:* Embeds invisible markers into media to verify authenticity and detect unauthorised alterations.
- *Digital signatures:* Encode cryptographic information derived from the media at the point of capture.

- *Device fingerprinting:* Uses unique characteristics of a recording device (e.g. lens distortion, sensor noise) to trace media to its source.
- *Blockchain-based provenance:* Logs media creation and modification events on an immutable ledger.
- *Trusted capture solutions:* Tools like Truepic and Serelay cryptographically bind metadata (e.g. time, location) to media at the point of capture.

Limitations include the need for active forensic techniques to have authentication data embedded in advance, making them incompatible with most consumer-grade devices and legacy content, and their inapplicability to the majority of online media, which typically lacks any form of embedded verification.

7.1.1.3 Provenance and Source Verification

Establishing the origin and history of media is a critical component of forensic authentication. Provenance verification helps determine whether content has been altered or misattributed. Examples include:

- *Reverse image and video search*: Tools like Google Reverse Image Search or InVID (a plugin toolkit designed to assist fact-checking through video verification) can trace media back to its earliest known appearance online.
- *Cryptographic hashing*: Hash values can be used to verify that a file has not been altered since its creation.
- *Content authentication networks*: Initiatives such as the C2PA aim to standardise metadata and provenance tracking across platforms.

Referring back to Figure 7.5, the AI-generated image of "a black cat drinking coffee" using M365 Copilot, built on the GPT-5 chat model. When the image is generated there are some values in the HEX data and text view "Open AI," "C2pa.claim.v2," and "TruePics Lens" that are not initially known to a creator. However, when the photo was edited using the AI feature of MS Paint and saved, a C2PA credentials tag was added and the user was alerted to this feature (Figure 7.7).

Figure 7.7 AI-generated image edited using AI (Microsoft Paint) – C2PA credentials added. Edited using Microsoft Paint (version 11.2512.191.0). AI Tool Attribution (if applicable): Image edited using Microsoft Paint (v.11.2512.191.0).

When MS Paint (both the classic version and the Windows 11 Paint with Cocreator AI edition) saves a file, it removes all metadata, and because these images are often created or downloaded online, this information is frequently absent from the outset.

Several additional indicators are worth noting: first, the total absence of metadata, as Paint consistently strips EXIF and XMP information, similar to many low-end editors. Second, re-encoding signatures, since Paint relies on Windows built-in codecs, which can produce predictable JPEG quantisation tables and characteristic recompression artefacts. And third, cropped or resized images that lack provenance metadata, resulting in "bare" files without expected camera tags, which can be a red flag in forensic analysis. These items of interest are illustrated in Figure 7.8.

Id	Name	Evidence Image Value	Evidence Image Warnings
1	Filename	Black Cat Coffee - Copy.png	
2	Full Path	C:\Users\cmpamacd\OneDrive -	
3	MD5	a2694bfdc9cf0b4e68375f4afcdd	
4	Decoded Pixels MD5	a3affddfb9303691f10ce97a67c3	
5	Format	PNG	Format is not a standard co
6	Format Description	Portable Network Graphics	
7	Image Encoded Size	1024 x 1536	
8	Image Displayed Size	1024 x 1536	
9	Image Normalized Size	1536 x 1024	
10	Aspect Ratio	1.50	
11	Number of Channels	4	Channels count different fr
12	BPP	32	BPP (32 different 24)
13	Thumbnail Size		Thumbnail is missing
14	Thumbnail Normalized Size		
15	Preview Size		
16	Preview Normalized Size		
17	Exif rotate tag		
18	Number of Exif fields	0	
19	Number of MakerNotes fields	0	
20	Number of IPTC fields	0	
21	Number of XMP fields	0	
22	Number of Photoshop fields	0	
23	Number of ICC fields	0	
24	Exif Make		EXIF Make is missing
25	Exif Model		EXIF Model is missing
26	Exif Software		

Figure 7.8 EXIF items of interest.

7.1.1.4 AI and Deep Learning-Based Detection

As deepfakes become more sophisticated, AI-based forensic techniques have emerged as a critical line of defence. These methods leverage machine learning to detect subtle artefacts and inconsistencies introduced during synthetic media generation. Key approaches include:

- *CNNs*: Trained to detect subtle artefacts in deepfakes, such as unnatural facial blending, inconsistent eye movement, or skin texture anomalies.
- *Temporal inconsistency analysis*: Evaluates frame-by-frame coherence in videos to detect unnatural transitions or motion artefacts.
- *Biometric verification*: Compares facial landmarks, lip-sync accuracy, and voice patterns against known biometric profiles to detect impersonation.

- *Multimodal analysis*: Cross-validates audio, video, and textual cues for semantic and temporal coherence, useful in detecting synthetic interviews or speeches.

Multimedia forensic authentication is a multidisciplinary field that combines signal processing, cryptography, machine learning, and metadata analysis to combat the growing threat of synthetic media. As deepfake technologies continue to advance, so too must the tools and strategies for verifying authenticity. A layered approach – combining passive, active, and AI-driven methods – is increasingly necessary to ensure robust and scalable media verification across industries.

7.2 Tooling Landscape: Enterprise and Open-Source Options

In addition to the forensic tools highlighted in Chapter 3, Table 3.1, other examples of Enterprise tools for detection and analysis include:

7.2.1 Magnet Verify

Magnet Verify is a specialised forensic tool designed to authenticate images and videos by detecting alterations, identifying file-integrity issues, and distinguishing genuine media from manipulated or AI-generated content. It goes beyond standard metadata checks by analysing provenance, tracing the originating device, and revealing editing history, providing investigators with reliable, court-admissible assessments of media authenticity. Its ability to identify tampering, confirm source information, and detect deepfakes makes it an essential resource for maintaining evidential integrity in modern digital investigations.

7.2.2 Oxygen Forensics

Oxygen Forensics integrates AI-driven analytics into its digital investigation ecosystem, with emerging capabilities for detecting deepfake content across multimedia evidence. The company emphasises the role of machine learning and multimodal analysis in identifying synthetic media within cloud and mobile environments. While Oxygen does not currently offer a dedicated deepfake detection module comparable to

Amped Authenticate, its roadmap includes leveraging AI for anomaly detection in video and audio streams, particularly in cases involving identity fraud and social engineering attacks. These developments align with broader forensic trends towards automated authenticity verification in distributed data environments.

7.2.3 Microsoft

In addition to Microsoft Video Authenticator, Microsoft approaches deepfake detection through a combination of provenance-based authentication and AI-driven analysis. Its Content Integrity Suite, developed under C2PA, enables creators to embed cryptographically verifiable metadata (known as Content Credentials) into digital assets. This mechanism allows subsequent tampering to be detected and traced, supporting transparency and trust in media ecosystems. These initiatives reflect Microsoft's dual strategy of technical detection and ecosystem-level standards to mitigate the risks posed by synthetic media.

7.2.4 Intel FakeCatcher

Intel FakeCatcher represents a pioneering approach to deepfake detection by leveraging biological signal analysis rather than conventional pixel-based or metadata-driven methods. It operates in real time, analysing subtle blood flow patterns in human faces captured in video frames – a physiological marker that generative models struggle to replicate accurately. This technique enables FakeCatcher to achieve detection accuracy rates of approximately 96%, making it suitable for high stakes applications such as media verification and social platform moderation. Its emphasis on non-invasive, real-time analysis positions it as a robust solution for combating synthetic video content at scale.

7.2.5 Sentinel

Sentinel adopts a machine learning-driven forensic workflow for detecting manipulated media. It provides both upload-based and API-integrated detection capabilities, allowing organisations to incorporate deepfake analysis into existing digital security infrastructures. Sentinel's system focuses on anomaly detection within visual and audio streams, supported by visualisation tools that highlight regions of suspected manipulation. While its detection accuracy depends on the complexity of the generative model used, Sentinel is widely recognised for its adaptability and integration potential in enterprise and government environments, making it a practical choice for operational deepfake mitigation.

The efficiency of deepfake detection tools can vary significantly due to differences in algorithmic design, supported modalities, and operational contexts. Many solutions remain monomodal, focusing on a single content type – such as video or image – rather than offering comprehensive multimodal analysis across audio, text, and visual streams. This limitation can reduce effectiveness in complex forensic scenarios where synthetic media spans multiple formats.

Furthermore, budgetary constraints and technical expertise play a critical role in deployment; advanced detection platforms often require substantial financial investment and specialised knowledge for configuration, interpretation, and integration into investigative workflows. Consequently, DFUs and organisations with limited resources may struggle to implement robust detection strategies, underscoring the need for scalable, user-friendly solutions that balance accuracy with accessibility.

7.2.6 Open-Source Tools

There are several open source deepfake detection tools that offer promising capabilities and can be integrated into existing forensic workflows. Frameworks such as DeepFaceLab, FaceForensics++, and Deepware Scanner (community edition) provide modular architectures that allow investigators to plug detection algorithms into broader digital forensic platforms. These tools often support API-based integration and can be customised for specific investigative needs, making them attractive for organisations seeking cost-effective alternatives to commercial products. While open-source solutions may require greater technical expertise for deployment and maintenance, their flexibility and community-driven development enable rapid adaptation to emerging generative models, positioning them as valuable components in hybrid forensic strategies (Table 7.3).

Table 7.3 Open-Source Forensic Tools

TOOL	CREATED DATE	KEY FEATURES	SUPPORTED MEDIA
DeepFaceLab	2019	Primarily for deepfake creation; useful for benchmarking detection models; supports GAN-based manipulations	Images and Videos
FaceForensics++	2019	Benchmark dataset and detection models; supports multiple manipulation techniques; widely used in academic research	Images and Videos
DFDC Challenge	2020	Pre-trained CNN/LSTM models for video detection; reproducible scripts; designed for large-scale benchmarking	Videos
DeeperForensics-1.0	2020	Large-scale dataset and detection benchmark; robust to adversarial attacks; supports multiple manipulation types	Images and Videos
Face X-ray	2020	Detects blending artefacts in facial regions; works well on low quality and compressed media	Images
FakeCatcher	2021	Detects deepfakes using biological signals (e.g. subtle blood flow patterns); real-time detection capability	Videos
Deepware Scanner	2021	Lightweight detection tool; API integration; focuses on detecting GAN-generated faces	Images
SeqDeepFake	2022	Sequential detection, PyTorch-based, focuses on temporal inconsistency analysis in videos	Videos
VideoForensicsNet	2022	CNN-based architecture optimised for video frame-level analysis; detects compression and blending artefacts	Videos
DeepSafe	2023	Multi-model support, image/video analysis, visualisation, GPU/CPU optimisation	Images, Videos
OpenFake	2025	Large-scale dataset (≈4M images) for benchmarking deepfake detection; crowdsourced adversarial platform for continual updates; strong generalisation to unseen generators	Image, Videos

Several established digital forensic platforms provide extensible architectures that allow for the integration of open source deepfake detection tools such as those in the above table, enabling investigators to enhance authenticity verification within broader workflows. For example:

Autopsy (by Sleuth Kit): Autopsy is an open-source forensic platform widely used for disk imaging and evidence analysis. Its modular plugin architecture supports the incorporation of custom scripts and detection algorithms. This flexibility enables investigators to embed deepfake detection modules for image and video authenticity checks during disk-level examinations, making it particularly useful in cases involving multimedia evidence recovered from storage devices.

Magnet AXIOM: Magnet AXIOM is a commercial forensic suite designed for comprehensive analysis of mobile, cloud, and computer data. It supports custom Python scripts and external tool integration, allowing practitioners to implement deepfake detection workflows alongside its native capabilities for artefact recovery and timeline reconstruction. This makes AXIOM suitable for multimedia examination in criminal investigations, where authenticity verification must occur alongside other digital evidence analysis.

FTK (Forensic Toolkit): FTK offers robust data processing and indexing capabilities for large-scale investigations. Through command-line automation and scripting, external detection tools can be integrated into FTK's workflow, enabling investigators to perform video and image authenticity verification during bulk evidence processing. This approach is particularly advantageous in enterprise or law enforcement environments handling high volumes of multimedia data.

X-Ways Forensics: X-Ways Forensics is known for its efficiency and scripting flexibility. Investigators can incorporate detection algorithms via its customisable scripting interface, facilitating advanced image analysis and metadata validation. This integration is valuable for forensic scenarios requiring granular examination of image properties and potential manipulation indicators.

Oxygen Forensic Detective: Oxygen Forensic Detective specialises in mobile and cloud data acquisition and analysis. Its API and plugin support enable seamless integration of open source deepfake detection models, allowing investigators to conduct multimedia authenticity checks within mobile and social media datasets. This capability is critical for cases involving identity fraud, social engineering, or disinformation campaigns.

7.3 Best Practices for Forensic and Investigative Response

Effective forensic and investigative responses to deepfake and fabricated media require a comprehensive approach that integrates technical, procedural, and collaborative strategies. Successful detection and analysis depend on advanced technologies combined with rigorous forensic methodologies.

7.3.1 Metadata Examination

Metadata examination is a critical step in digital forensic investigations, as it involves analysing the hidden data embedded within files to uncover details about their origin, history, and potential tampering. Metadata can provide valuable insights into *how*, *when*, and *by whom* a file was created or modified, making it an essential tool for verifying authenticity and detecting manipulation (Table 7.4).

Table 7.4 Metadata Examination Tool Examples

TOOL	FUNCTIONALITY	EXAMPLE
Autopsy	Analyse the file's metadata, hash values, and file-system artefacts recovered from a suspect's device.	Traces of image manipulation applications or detects workflow artefacts associated with synthetic-media generation, may indicate deepfake involvement.
ExifTool	Reads metadata from diverse formats (JPEG, PNG, PDF, etc. offering insights into EXIF data and file properties.	A photo circulating online that appears to show a public figure may contain EXIF data listing "AI Generator" or may lack the sensor-specific noise profile expected from a real camera, supporting the hypothesis that the image is a deepfake.
Amped Authenticate	Specialised in forensic image authentication. Performs error-level analysis, noise pattern evaluation, recompression analysis, PRNU (sensor fingerprinting), and detection of editing-software artefacts.	Investigators analysing a suspicious portrait may find inconsistent noise patterns or recompression traces that do not match genuine camera output. Authenticate may also detect signatures of editing software used in deepfake workflows, indicating the image has been manipulated.
MediaInfo	Extracts detailed technical metadata from audio and video files, including codec info, encoding settings, bitrates, frame rates, colour space, and container structure.	A video submitted as "raw evidence" may be shown by MediaInfo to have been transcoded recently – suggesting that it may have passed through an AI generator or editing pipeline typical of deepfake production.

TOOL	FUNCTIONALITY	EXAMPLE
FotoForensics / ELA Tools	Provides quick online screening for metadata anomalies, ELA, and compression-layer inconsistencies. Useful for rapid triage of suspicious media.	A photo shared on social media may show uneven compression layers or pixel-level artefacts when uploaded to an online ELA tool (early indicators that the image could be AI-generated or heavily manipulated).

The above tools' ability to extract and correlate image artefacts across storage allows investigators to identify whether the media originated from the device, was downloaded from an external source, or was created using editing or generative AI software.

7.3.1.1 Best Practice Workflow

1. *Evidence acquisition and preservation*
    - Secure the original file: Always work on verified copies, never the original.
    - Verify integrity: Use cryptographic hashing (MD5, SHA-256) to ensure the file remains unaltered.
    - Document chain of custody: Record who handled the file, when, and how.

2. *Initial file assessment*
    - Identify file type and format: Images (JPEG, PNG), video (MP4, MOV), audio (WAV, MP3).
    - Check for anomalies: Unexpected file sizes, unusual extensions, or non-standard headers.

3. *Metadata analysis*
    - Use multiple tools: Examples include ExifTool, MediaInfo, and custom forensic utilities.
    - Capture all available metadata:
        - o File creation and modification timestamps
        - o Device and software identifiers (camera model, app versions)
        - o Geolocation and GPS tags
        - o Encoding and compression details
    - Look for inconsistencies:
        - o Mismatched software versions or unusual camera models

- o Timestamps that contradict the claimed timeline
- o Metadata patterns inconsistent with the file type or source

- Cross-reference with known AI/deepfake signatures:
  - o Many AI-generation tools leave detectable traces in metadata, such as software-specific markers or missing EXIF fields.
- Correlate with external evidence: Compare with other media, social accounts, or corroborating information to identify discrepancies.

4. *Documentation and reporting*

   - Maintain a complete audit trail: Record all extraction methods, software versions, and analysis steps.
   - Visualise key findings: Tables or timelines highlighting suspicious metadata can improve clarity.
   - Report limitations: Note when metadata may be missing, altered, or unreliable, and avoid over-interpretation.

5. *Preservation for future analysis*

   - Store all extracted metadata and working files securely
   - Ensure reproducibility: Another analyst should be able to replicate your findings using the documented workflow.
   - Update methods as AI evolves: New deepfake tools may strip, alter, or obfuscate metadata, so continuous monitoring of AI trends is essential.

7.3.2 Frame-by-Frame Inspection (Video Forensics)

Frame-by-frame inspection perform a meticulous visual review of individual video frames to uncover anomalies that automated detection tools may miss. This process, whether manual or semi-automated, involves examining each frame in detail to identify subtle signs of manipulation, inconsistencies, or artefacts introduced during editing or fabrication. Automated algorithms typically focus on broad patterns or compression artefacts, but advanced forgeries (such as deepfakes or spliced footage) often contain only minor irregularities in specific frames. Careful human-led analysis can reveal these subtle discrepancies, providing critical evidence of tampering.

Tables 7.5 and 7.6 outline key aspects to examine during frame-by-frame deepfake analysis, followed by a selection of suitable forensic tools that can be used to investigate these anomalies effectively.

Table 7.5 Frame-by-Frame Outliers

ASPECT	WHAT TO LOOK FOR	EXAMPLE
Lighting and Shadows	Examine whether the direction, intensity, and colour temperature of lighting remain consistent across consecutive frames. Look for shadows that flicker, disappear, or change shape unexpectedly. Deepfake generators often struggle with multi-source lighting, reflective surfaces, and soft shadow behaviour over time.	A subject walking through a room maintains consistent overhead lighting, but in one frame their cast shadow shifts sideways or vanishes entirely, suggesting synthetic reconstruction of that frame.
Facial Features and Expressions	Check for unnatural facial transitions, inconsistent muscle movement, mismatched blink rates, or desynchronised eye tracking. Subtle artefacts may appear around the mouth during speech or when the face turns quickly. Deepfakes may also exhibit temporal instability—small facial details changing frame to frame.	The person smiles naturally across several frames, but during a rapid head turn the facial geometry briefly collapses, or the mouth movement fails to synchronise with the audio, revealing a generation error.
Background Details	Inspect background objects, reflections, and textures for continuity. Deepfakes often reconstruct only the foreground face, leading to accidental warping, shifting patterns, or inconsistencies behind the subject. Reflections in glass or metal are especially telling because AI models frequently ignore them.	A logo on a wall stays fixed for most of the clip, but in two frames it shifts position or warps slightly, indicating that the background was not consistently reconstructed.
Compression Artefacts	Look for irregular blockiness, pixel clusters, colour banding, or blurred patches that appear only around the manipulated region. Sudden changes in compression pattern between frames—especially around the face—can signal that these areas were regenerated or blended.	A video appears normally compressed overall, but around the face region only, heavy block artefacts pulse or crawl between frames, suggesting the deepfake generator re-encoded just that region.
Reflections and Highlights	Check reflections on eyeglasses, jewellery, windows, or polished surfaces. Deepfakes often fail to re-create accurate reflection behaviour or consistent highlight positions, especially during rapid movements.	The subject's glasses reflect window light in most frames, but in several frames the reflection is missing or incorrectly positioned, suggesting the glasses region was partially reconstructed.

Table 7.6 Forensic Tools for Frame-by-Frame Analysis

TOOL	FUNCTIONALITY
Amped FIVE	Amped FIVE is a professional, court-accepted forensic software suite specifically designed for image and video analysis. It provides precise frame-by-frame navigation, allowing analysts to examine micro-level temporal inconsistencies that often indicate deepfake generation errors. The platform includes a wide range of enhancement tools (such as deblurring, stabilisation, noise reduction, colour correction, and geometric adjustments) that can reveal subtle artefacts concealed in manipulated footage. Its measurement and annotation capabilities allow forensic examiners to mark anomalies, compare sequences, and prepare visually clear evidential reports. Amped FIVE preserves forensic soundness and maintains a full audit trail, valuable for preparing evidence for legal proceedings involving suspected deepfake media.
VLC Media Player	VLC is a lightweight, widely accessible media player that includes basic but useful forensic features, such as frame-by-frame stepping, playback speed reduction, looping segments, and screenshot extraction. While it is not designed as a forensic tool, it is highly effective for quick triage and preliminary inspection of suspected deepfakes. Analysts can rapidly scan for visual inconsistencies, such as flickering artefacts, boundary mismatches, or unnatural transitions, without having to load the file into more complex systems. Because VLC supports almost every video codec and container format, it is often the first tool used to preview evidence safely and without altering metadata.
FFmpeg	FFmpeg is a powerful command-line toolkit widely used in digital forensics for extracting frames, analysing encoding parameters, and converting media into formats suitable for structured examination. For deepfake investigations, FFmpeg is ideal for generating frame sequences that can be inspected individually or compared side-by-side. Investigators can export entire videos as high-resolution still images, isolate specific intervals, or re-encode footage to preserve original quality during analysis. Additionally, FFmpeg can reveal technical details about the encoding pipeline (such as bitrate anomalies, unusual GOP structures, or inconsistent frame metadata) which may indicate synthetic generation or tampering. Its automation capabilities make it an indispensable tool for large-scale or batch-based frame analysis.
Adobe Premiere Pro / DaVinci Resolve	Although primarily designed for video editing, Adobe Premiere Pro and DaVinci Resolve can support forensic review when integrated into forensic workflows. Their advanced timeline interfaces allow analysts to examine footage with precision, scrubbing frame by frame to detect temporal instability characteristic of deepfakes. Both suites offer sophisticated colour grading, zooming, masking, and playback analysis tools that help magnify subtle inconsistencies in lighting, facial geometry, or background behaviour.

7.3.2.1 Best Practice Workflow

1. *Preserve original media*
   Always work on a copy of the file while maintaining the original in its untouched state. This ensures integrity and supports chain of custody for legal admissibility.
2. *Extract frames*
   Use tools like FFmpeg to convert the video into an image sequence. This allows detailed inspection of individual frames without compression artefacts introduced by repeated playback.
3. *Initial screening*
   Perform a quick review using simple tools such as VLC Media Player to step through frames manually. Look for obvious anomalies like sudden lighting changes or missing shadows.
4. *Detailed visual analysis*
   Examine each frame closely for forensic indicators:
   - Lighting and shadow inconsistencies
   - Unnatural facial transitions or mismatched eye movements
   - Background shifts or texture changes
   - Localised compression artefacts around manipulated regions
5. *Apply forensic enhancements*
   Use professional tools like Amped FIVE to zoom, clarify, and annotate suspicious areas. Amped FIVE's forensic filters help reveal subtle artefacts that may indicate deepfake generation or manipulation.
6. *Metadata verification*
   Check frame-level metadata using ExifTool or MediaInfo. Look for anomalies in timestamps, encoding details, or evidence of recompression and editing software.
7. *Contextual verification*
   Cross-reference the video with authentic sources, corroborate events, and assess plausibility. Technical findings should be supported by contextual checks.
8. *Document findings*

   Record every step, including methodology, tools, settings, and annotated frames. Comprehensive documentation ensures reproducibility and strengthens legal admissibility.

7.3.3 Audio Forensics

Audio forensics involves the scientific analysis of voice recordings to verify authenticity, detect tampering, and identify synthetic or manipulated speech. This process is critical in cases involving voice evidence, as audio can be easily edited or generated using advanced AI tools. Key areas to examine and items of interest are shown in Table 7.7.

Table 7.7 Audio Forensic Indicators

ASPECT	WHAT TO LOOK FOR	EXAMPLE
Pitch and Tone Irregularities	Listen for sudden, unexplained shifts in pitch, timbre, resonance, or vocal brightness. Natural human speech contains smooth micro-variations influenced by breath, emotion, and physiology; deepfakes or spliced audio often introduce abrupt tonal jumps or inconsistent resonance. These anomalies may occur when segments from different recordings (or AI-generated fragments) are stitched together.	A speaker begins a sentence with a warm, full tone, but halfway through a word the voice abruptly becomes thinner or changes resonance, suggesting either synthesis or splicing.
Unnatural Pauses and Timing	Pay close attention to the pacing and rhythm of speech. Human speakers follow natural breathing cycles, pausing predictably for emphasis or inhalation. Deepfakes may introduce timing inconsistencies such as unnaturally long silences, clipped breaths, or sudden pace changes. These can indicate inserted synthetic segments or poorly aligned edits.	A conversation flows normally, but a pause appears in a place where no natural breath would occur, or a phrase starts too quickly after another, breaking natural conversational cadence.
Synthetic Speech Patterns	AI-generated voices often lack micro-irregularities – small pitch wobbles, subtle hesitations, and natural texture. Instead, they may sound overly smooth, rhythmically uniform, or slightly robotic. Watch for intonational patterns that seem repetitive or too consistent across multiple sentences, as many TTS systems reuse prosodic templates (pre-defined, structured representations of prosodic features, e.g. pitch contour, energy/loudness, and rhythm).	Speech sounds unusually steady, with perfectly even pacing and identical intonation patterns across multiple sentences, lacking the natural imperfections found in human vocal delivery.
Background Noise Consistency	Examine whether ambient noise remains continuous and stable across the recording. In genuine audio, background hum, environmental noise, and room reverberation remain relatively constant. Splicing or AISynth-generated speech often disrupts this continuity—background hum may cut, shift, or momentarily vanish when synthetic segments are inserted.	A faint cooling fan hum is audible throughout: except for a few seconds when the speaker gives a key statement, during which the hum suddenly disappears before returning.

Appropriate audio forensic tools and their functionalities are outlined in Table 7.8.

Table 7.8 Audio Forensic Tools

TOOL	DESCRIPTION
Amped Authenticate (Audio Module)	Amped Authenticate's audio module provides forensic specialists with tools to detect editing traces, recompression artefacts, and discontinuities that may indicate tampering or synthetic voice insertion. It can analyse waveform irregularities, examine encoding signatures, and identify abrupt transitions inconsistent with natural recording processes. This makes it particularly useful for uncovering audio splicing, voice-cloning artefacts, and anomalies introduced by deepfake generation pipelines. Its structured reporting and forensic-sound workflow ensure results can be used confidently in investigative or legal settings.
iZotope RX	iZotope RX is a professional-grade audio restoration and forensic suite equipped with powerful modules for noise reduction, spectral repair, de-reverberation, and dialogue isolation. In deepfake analysis, its detailed spectrogram view, frequency-specific enhancement, and audio fingerprinting capabilities allow analysts to isolate subtle anomalies—such as synthetic harmonics, unnatural smoothing, or abrupt tonal shifts introduced by AI synthesis. RX can also separate background noise and vocal elements, making inconsistencies between layers more visible and helping investigators identify machine-generated speech artefacts that would otherwise be difficult to detect.
Praat	Praat is a widely used open-source tool for phonetic and linguistic analysis, enabling detailed examination of pitch contours, formant frequencies, amplitude variation, and voice-quality parameters. For deepfake detection, Praat allows analysts to observe micro-prosodic features, such as jitter, shimmer, and natural pitch fluctuations, which are often smoothed out or inconsistently replicated in synthetic voices. Its visualisation of formant trajectories can reveal whether speech maintains physiologically plausible patterns or displays artificial stability or abrupt changes, both characteristic of AI-generated speech.
Spectrogram Analysis Tools, e.g. Audacity, Sonic Visualiser	Spectrogram-based tools provide a visual representation of frequency, amplitude, and time, making them essential for identifying irregularities that might not be audible. Audacity offers accessible spectrogram views and basic filters, while Sonic Visualiser provides more advanced overlays, peak analysis, and time-frequency decomposition. In deepfake forensics, spectrograms can reveal unnatural harmonic structures, inconsistent background noise, missing breath markers, or artefacts such as "spectral smearing" associated with neural vocoders. These visual cues help analysts differentiate genuine human speech patterns from synthetic or manipulated audio.

7.3.3.1 Best Practice Workflow

Best practices emphasise maintaining integrity, documentation, and using a systematic approach. A comprehensive workflow for audio forensic analysis is presented as follows:

1. *Evidence acquisition and preservation*
   - Secure the original recording – work only on verified forensic copies.
   - Document the chain of custody.
   - Use cryptographic hashes (e.g. MD5, SHA-256) to verify that copies are identical.

2. *Initial assessment*
   - Determine the context and purpose of analysis (e.g. authentication, speaker identification, enhancement).
   - Assess the recording's format (i.e. sample rate, bit depth, compression).
   - Identify potential issues such as noise, distortion, overlaps, or gaps that may affect reliability or indicate possible manipulation.

3. *Preparation*
   - Convert to a lossless format (e.g. WAV) for analysis.
   - Segment relevant portions, while keeping full evidence intact.
   - Maintain a detailed log of all steps (software versions, settings, etc.).

4. *Forensic analysis*
   - Authentication: Look for edits or tampering via spectrograms, waveform, metadata, and possibly electrical-network frequency (ENF) analysis (fluctuating background hums).
   - Speaker identification: Use acoustic analysis (pitch, formants), manual listening and, where allowed, automated tools.
   - Enhancement/clarification: Apply noise reduction carefully, only to improve intelligibility (avoid destructive processing).

5. *Documentation*
   - Keep a full audit trail: every action, setting, and decision must be documented.
   - Use visual aids (i.e. waveforms, spectrograms) to illustrate findings.

- Ensure reproducibility: another qualified analyst should be able to replicate your process.

6. *Reporting*

   - Write a clear, understandable report, avoiding unnecessary jargon.
   - Describe your methodology, tools, and settings.
   - Provide annotated examples (e.g. waveform snippets, spectrograms, transcripts).

7.3.4 Use of AI and Machine Learning Tools

AI and machine learning have become essential in modern forensic workflows for detecting sophisticated media manipulations. These tools leverage algorithms trained on large datasets to identify subtle inconsistencies that are often imperceptible to the human eye or traditional forensic methods. Key detection capabilities include:

- *Facial movement analysis:*
  AI models track micro-expressions, eye blinks, and head movements to detect unnatural patterns. *Example*: A deepfake video where the eye-blinking frequency is abnormally low compared to natural human behaviour.
- *Lip-sync verification:*
  Algorithms compare audio and visual streams to ensure speech aligns with mouth movements. *Example*: Detecting mismatched lip movements in a fabricated interview clip.
- *Voice modulation detection:*
  ML-based audio analysis identifies synthetic speech or pitch anomalies indicative of voice cloning. *Example*: Spotting overly smooth intonation in AI-generated voices.
- *Lighting and shadow consistency:*
  AI tools analyse pixel-level lighting patterns to detect inconsistencies across frames. *Example*: A subject's shadow direction changes abruptly in a spliced video (Table 7.9).

Table 7.9 AI/Machine Learning Tools

TOOL	DESCRIPTION
Microsoft Video Authenticator	Microsoft Video Authenticator is an AI-driven forensic tool designed to analyse videos and still images for signs of deepfake manipulation. It works by detecting subtle artefacts (such as blended edges, abnormal fading, or inconsistencies in facial textures) that are typically invisible to the human eye. The system produces a confidence score estimating the likelihood that the media has been artificially generated. Although originally developed to combat election-related misinformation, it is increasingly used in forensic workflows to flag potentially manipulated videos for further manual examination.
Deepware Scanner	Deepware Scanner uses deep learning models to evaluate videos for traces of AI-generated content. It identifies patterns characteristic of deepfake algorithms, such as irregular facial warping, inconsistent frame-to-frame rendering, and latent artefacts created by generative models. The tool is particularly effective for rapid screening, allowing investigators, journalists, and security teams to filter large volumes of media and highlight high-risk clips for more detailed forensic review.
Amber Video	Amber Video provides real-time deepfake detection by analysing incoming video streams frame by frame. Its algorithms monitor facial movement, blink rates, texture coherence, and temporal stability to spot signs of synthetic generation as the video plays. This makes it especially useful for live broadcast environments, remote interviews, verification of video submissions, and defence against real-time impersonation attacks. Its instant feedback capability helps prevent the circulation of manipulated footage before it spreads.
Resemble Detect	Resemble Detect is a specialised tool for identifying synthetic or cloned voices. Using machine-learning models trained on vocal characteristics, it compares speech samples against patterns typical of AI-generated audio. The system flags anomalies such as unnatural smoothness, missing micro-prosodic variations, or mismatched formant structures. This makes it valuable in cases involving voice-cloning fraud, synthetic phone scams, and authentication of spoken evidence, offering investigators a targeted solution for detecting audio deepfakes.

7.3.4.1 Best Practice Workflow

The best practice workflow for AI-assisted media forensics involves four key stages. First, pre-processing is undertaken to extract relevant video frames and audio segments in a controlled, reproducible manner. Next, AI models are applied to these materials, using state-of-the-art deepfake detection algorithms across both visual and auditory streams. The resulting outputs are then cross-verified through established forensic techniques, including metadata analysis and detailed frame-by-frame inspection, to ensure findings are corroborated by independent evidence. Finally, all outcomes are carefully reported, with confidence scores, anomaly descriptions, and any limitations of the models clearly documented. Throughout the entire workflow, rigorous documentation of actions, transparent methodological notes, and attention to model explainability are essential to maintain auditability, support expert interpretation, and ensure results can withstand professional or legal scrutiny.

Together, these techniques form a comprehensive approach to verifying the authenticity of digital content and are foundational to any forensic or investigative response to deepfake threats. These methods vary in scope, from analysing metadata and file structure to using machine learning classifiers and visual anomaly detection techniques.

7.3.5 Human-on-the-Loop and Four-Eyes Principle in AI Governance

The "Human-on-the-Loop" paradigm ensures that automated systems operate under continuous human oversight, particularly in high-risk domains such as forensic AI and cybersecurity. Unlike "human-in-the-loop," which requires direct intervention before execution, human-on-the-loop allows automation to function autonomously while enabling humans to monitor, override, or audit decisions when necessary. This approach mitigates risks associated with algorithmic bias, adversarial attacks, and false positives in deepfake detection systems [9, 10].

Complementing this, the "Four-Eyes Principle" mandates that critical decisions undergo review by at least two qualified individuals, reinforcing accountability and reducing the likelihood of unilateral errors. In forensic workflows, this principle is particularly relevant when validating authenticity assessments or approving evidence for legal proceedings. Together, these governance strategies create a layered control model that balances operational efficiency with ethical and legal safeguards, ensuring transparency and trust in AI-driven processes [11].

7.4 Collaborative Efforts Between Law Enforcement, Technology Companies, and Policymakers

The increasing sophistication of deepfake technologies has created an urgent need for coordinated cross-sector responses. Effective mitigation of synthetic media threats requires collaboration between law enforcement agencies, technology developers, and policymakers. These partnerships are essential for developing robust strategies to detect, investigate, and respond to manipulated digital content.

At the forefront of this effort are digital forensic experts, who continuously refine analytical techniques and machine learning algorithms to improve detection accuracy. Their work involves a detailed examination of facial micro-expressions, vocal tone and cadence, lighting and shadow inconsistencies, and other subtle indicators of manipulation. However, staying ahead of malicious actors demands more than technical innovation - it requires sustained interdisciplinary cooperation.

Researchers contribute cutting-edge solutions, law enforcement brings operational insights from real-world cases, and policymakers shape regulatory frameworks that ensure ethical and effective deployment of these technologies. Together, these stakeholders form a critical alliance to safeguard the integrity of digital media and protect individuals, institutions, and democratic processes from the harmful consequences of synthetic content.

A notable example of such collaboration is the Deepfake Detection Challenge, launched in the UK in 2024. This joint initiative – led by the Home Office, the Department for Science, Innovation and Technology (DSIT), the Alan Turing Institute, and the Accelerated Capability Environment (ACE) – unites academia, industry, and government to address the deepfake threat through innovation and shared expertise.

In addition, since 2021 Liverpool John Moores University (LJMU) has partnered with Merseyside Police to combat deepfake-related crime, introduced the MSc in Audio and Video Forensics. Developed by LJMU's School of Engineering in consultation with Merseyside Police, this programme addresses both audio and video aspects of deepfake media. It combines advanced technical training with practical forensic methodologies, equipping students with the expertise needed to meet emerging challenges in digital forensics.

7.4.1 Proactive Prevention

While detection remains critical, the next frontier in combating deepfakes is proactive prevention via embedding resilience directly into media assets and training data to disrupt synthetic content generation at its source. Two promising approaches are adversarial watermarking and AI poisoning, which introduce adversarial noise or misleading signals into generative models, degrading the quality and reliability of deepfakes. Recent research demonstrates practical implementations of these concepts:

Adversarial watermarking
Adversarial watermarking is a proactive forensic strategy that embeds imperceptible signals into media to strengthen provenance tracking and enhance detection robustness. Unlike traditional watermarking, which focuses solely on copyright protection, adversarial watermarking leverages perturbations that exploit vulnerabilities in deepfake generation and detection pipelines. These perturbations are optimised to act as adversarial signals, improving detection accuracy without degrading visual quality. Recent studies demonstrate that adversarial watermarking can significantly interfere with deep neural networks by adjusting watermark parameters (such as transparency, size, and position), through gradient-based optimisation, thereby reducing misclassification confidence in target models while maintaining human-perceptible integrity. This approach not only aids in identifying forged content but also introduces resilience against evasion attacks by embedding security at the media level [12, 13].

Invisible and secure watermark perturbations (ISWP)
ISWP combines adversarial attack principles with invisible watermarking to embed perturbations that mislead generative models while preserving copyright and authenticity. Techniques often employ frequency-domain transformations such as the Discrete Wavelet Transform (DWT) and encryption-based embedding to create imperceptible distortions. These distortions degrade the fidelity of deepfake outputs when tampered with, effectively sabotaging synthesis pipelines. By integrating cryptographic security with adversarial robustness, ISWP ensures that watermarks remain undetectable to humans yet disruptive to AI-driven manipulation.

Watermark-embedded adversarial examples for diffusion models
Zhao et al. [14] proposed embedding personal watermarks into adversarial examples to force diffusion models (used in

image generation) to output visibly watermarked content, preventing unauthorised imitation and reducing the usability of generated deepfakes. By coupling adversarial optimisation with watermark embedding, this approach introduces a dual-layer defence: preserving ownership while degrading the quality of synthetic outputs.

Data poisoning tools
Nightshade [15, 16], developed by researchers at the University of Chicago, exemplifies a preventive strategy that targets the training phase of generative models. It introduces pixel-level perturbations invisible to humans but disruptive to AI learning. When poisoned images are scraped into training datasets, they corrupt the model's internal representations, causing chaotic outputs (such as mislabelling dogs as cats), thereby undermining the reliability of deepfake generation pipelines. This technique highlights the growing importance of dataset-level defences in combating synthetic media proliferation.

These strategies represent a paradigm shift from reactive detection to proactive prevention, embedding security signals into content and poisoning training data to undermine malicious generative models. Coupled with robust forensic standards and international collaboration, these approaches can significantly strengthen global defences against deepfake threats.

7.4.2 Developing a Deepfake-Specific Forensic Process Model

To support consistent and legally sound investigations, a dedicated forensic process model for deepfake analysis should be developed in consultation with law enforcement and digital forensic practitioners. This model should address the full lifecycle of synthetic media in investigations, including:

- Detection and initial triage
- Acquisition and preservation
- Validation and analysis
- Documentation and reporting
- Evidentiary handling and legal compliance

An example of such a framework is the Surrey and Sussex Police Deepfake Technology Policy [17], which outlines a structured approach to verifying the authenticity of crime-related media: including CCTV footage, video recordings, audio files, and still images. The policy integrates technical detection methods with operational procedures, ensuring that suspected synthetic content is handled in a way that maintains evidential integrity. Its significance lies in bridging forensic rigour with procedural clarity, offering law enforcement a practical and legally compliant roadmap for managing deepfake-related cases.

7.4.3 Real-Time Strategies for Verifying Media Authenticity

The rise of deepfakes and other forms of media manipulation presents a growing challenge for organisations, particularly due to the ease of creation and rapid dissemination of synthetic content. User-friendly generative tools now allow attackers with minimal technical expertise to produce highly convincing media, which can be distributed across multiple channels (including email, voice calls, and social platforms) at speed. These attacks are often amplified through social media networks and exploit psychological vulnerabilities, especially in urgent or emotionally charged scenarios (e.g. "CEO requires immediate bank transfer"), where individuals are less likely to question authenticity.

Humans are naturally predisposed to trust familiar faces and voices, a tendency that deepfakes exploit to make fabricated content appear genuine. The widespread use of digital communication platforms such as Teams, Zoom, and email has further normalised remote interactions, reducing scepticism towards seemingly routine requests. Emerging technologies now enable real-time manipulation of faces and voices during live interactions, complicating detection in contexts such as virtual meetings, remote onboarding, and identity verification.

To build resilience against synthetic media, organisations and agencies should adopt the following strategies:

- *Interdisciplinary teams*: Combine expertise from law enforcement, cybersecurity, academia, and media ethics. Embedding deepfake detection into academic curricula fosters critical evaluation of current tools and supports the development of robust forensic methodologies. Collaboration with local DFUs ensures that research is grounded in operational realities.

- *Regular training*: Equip investigators and analysts with up-to-date knowledge of emerging deepfake technologies, detection tools, and forensic workflows.
- *Information sharing networks*: Participate in national and international forums to exchange threat intelligence, case studies, and best practices.

In addition, to mitigate these risks, organisations must adopt a multi-layered strategy for real-time media verification. This includes:

- Integrating AI-driven detection tools into content pipelines to identify synthetic artefacts. Solutions such as Microsoft's Video Authenticator, Intel's FakeCatcher, and Deepware Scanner offer real-time analysis of visual and auditory cues to flag potential deepfakes.
- Implementing incident response playbooks that outline procedures for managing deepfake-related events. These should include protocols for issuing public statements, initiating takedown requests, preserving evidence, and pursuing legal remedies.
- Adopting content provenance and watermarking standards, such as those developed by the C2PA, to embed cryptographic metadata that verifies the origin and integrity of media assets.
- Deploying biometric and liveness detection protocols during video calls or identity checks. Techniques such as dynamic facial recognition (e.g. blinking, head movements) help detect static or pre-recorded deepfakes.
- Utilising AI-based detection models trained to identify inconsistencies in visual and auditory signals, such as lighting anomalies, irregular skin textures, unnatural eye movements, or pitch variations in voice recordings.

7.4.4 Policy Documentation and Workflows

To support these technical measures, organisations should establish clear policies and best practices for addressing the threat of synthetic media. These policies should:

- Educate employees about the risks associated with deepfakes and fabricated content.

- Define procedures for verifying the authenticity of digital media.
- Provide clear steps for reporting suspicious materials or incidents.

Deepfake awareness training, secure content-sharing protocols, and standardised communication practices can significantly reduce the risk of misinformation, reputational damage, and security breaches. A proactive deepfake policy not only protects organisational integrity but also empowers employees to respond confidently and responsibly when confronted with deceptive media.

It is equally important to develop best practice workflows and reference use-cases tailored to specific industry sectors. Each sector faces unique risks and operational challenges related to synthetic media. Sector-specific workflows should define:

- Verification procedures appropriate to the context.
- Response actions and escalation pathways.
- Roles and responsibilities for managing suspected deepfake incidents.

For example, media organisations may implement rigorous source authentication and editorial review protocols, while financial institutions might prioritise identity verification and fraud prevention. By designing customised workflows, organisations ensure that employees have practical, context-relevant guidance, improving preparedness and consistency in responding to emerging digital threats.

7.5 Summary

In confronting the escalating threat of deepfakes, a multifaceted approach that combines technological innovation, policy development, and public awareness is essential. This chapter has explored the evolving landscape of detection tools, authentication methods, and strategic interventions designed to mitigate the risks posed by synthetic media. While no single solution offers complete protection, the integration of AI-driven detection systems, robust digital provenance mechanisms, and cross-sector collaboration provides a resilient defence. Ultimately, addressing the deepfake challenge requires not only technical ingenuity but also a sustained commitment to ethical standards, education, and global cooperation. As the technology continues to advance, so too must our strategies—ensuring that truth, trust, and transparency remain at the core of our digital ecosystems.

References

[1] B. M. Le, J. Kim, S. S. Woo, K. Moore, A. Abuadbba, and S. Tariq, 'SoK: Systematization and benchmarking of deepfake detectors in a unified framework', *ArXiv*, no. 2401.04364, Mar. 2025. Available: http://arxiv.org/abs/2401.04364

[2] Á. MacDermott, 'Deepfake forensics: Exploring the impact and implications of fabricated media in digital forensic investigations – DFRWS EU poster', in *Digital Forensics Research Workshop Europe (DFRWS EU 2025). Brno, Czech Republic*, 2025. Accessed: Apr. 03, 2025. Available: https://dfrws.org/wp-content/uploads/2025/04/DFRWS_EU_2025_paperposter_115.pdf

[3] Á. MacDermott, 'Deepfake forensic survey dataset', Liverpool John Moores University. Dataset available via JISC. LJMU Ethics Approval Reference: 25/CMP/004., Oct. 2025.

[4] S. Singh and A. Dhumane, 'Unmasking digital deceptions: An integrative review of deepfake detection, multimedia forensics, and cybersecurity challenges', Dec. 01, 2025, Elsevier B.V. doi: 10.1016/j.mex.2025.103632.

[5] P. Capasso, G. Cattaneo, and M. de Marsico, 'A comprehensive survey on methods for image integrity", *ACM Transactions on Multimedia Computing, Communications and Applications*, vol. 20, no. 11, Sep. 2024, doi: 10.1145/3633203.

[6] I. Amerini *et al.* 'Deepfake media forensics: Status and future challenges', *Journal of Imaging*, vol. 11, no. 3, Mar. 2025, doi: 10.3390/jimaging11030073.

[7] B. Carrier, *File System Forensic Analysis*. Addison-Wesley, 2005.

[8] J. Williams, 'Tackling AI threats: Advanced DFIR methods and tools for deepfake detection', *Pen Test Partners*, Jan, 2025. Available: www.pentestpartners.com/security-blog/tackling-ai-threats-advanced-dfir-methods-and-tools-for-deepfake-detection/.

[9] European Commission, '*EU Artificial Intelligence Act: Regulatory Framework for Trustworthy AI*', European Union, Jul. 2024.

[10] M. Malatji, 'Augmented intelligence framework for human–artificial intelligence teaming in cybersecurity', *Human-Centric Intelligent Systems*, vol. 5, no. 2, pp. 1–30, Jun. 2025.

[11] United Nations Industrial Development Organization, 'What is the four-eyes principle?', UNIDO, Available: www.unido.org/overview/member-states/change-management/faq/what-four-eyes-principle.

[12] Y. Yao, A. Jain, and S. Liu, 'Adversarial watermarking for face recognition', *arXiv: 2409. 16056*, no. v1, pp. 1–8, Sep. 2024. Available: http://arxiv.org/abs/2409.16056

[13] G. Wang, Xinyuan Chen, and Chang Xu, '2018 IEEE international conference on acoustics, speech and signal processing: Proceedings: April 15–20, 2018, Calgary Telus Convention Center, Calgary, Alberta, Canada', in *ICASSP 2019–2019 IEEE International Conference on Acoustics, Speech and Signal Processing (ICASSP)*, IEEE, Apr. 2019, pp. 1962–1966.

[14] Y. Cui, J. Ren, H. Xu, P. He, H. Liu, L. Sun, Y. Xing, and J. Tang 'DiffusionShield: A watermark for data copyright protection against generative diffusion models', *ACM SIGKDD explorations newsletter*, vol. 26, no. 2, pp. 60–75

[15] Glaze Project, 'What is nightshade?', *The Glaze Project*. Available: https://nightshade.cs.uchicago.edu/whatis.html.

[16] S. Shan, W. Ding, J. Passananti, S. Wu, H. Zheng, and B. Y. Zhao, 'Nightshade: Prompt-specific poisoning attacks on text-to-image generative models', Apr. 2024. Available: http://arxiv.org/abs/2310.13828

[17] Surrey Police and Sussex Police, 'Deepfake Technology Policy (Surrey and Sussex) (1241)', Nov. 25, 2024. Available: www.sussex.police.uk/SysSiteAssets/foi-media/sussex/policies/deepfake-technology-policy-surrey-and-sussex-1241.pdf.

8
The Future of Digital Forensics in the Age of Deepfakes

Having established the scope, impact, and challenges posed by deepfakes throughout this book, this concluding chapter turns towards the future of digital forensics in an increasingly synthetic landscape. As AI and machine learning continue to advance, they offer both new tools for forensic analysis and new threats to evidentiary integrity. This chapter explores how these technologies are reshaping forensic capabilities, prompting a re-evaluation of traditional methodologies to meet the demands of a future where digital deception is more sophisticated and pervasive. We also examine emerging directions in research and practice, including mapping deepfake incidents, understanding practitioner perspectives, assessing the hidden prevalence of manipulated media, and identifying open questions that will define the next frontier of digital forensic science.

8.1 Advancements in AI and Machine Learning for Forensic Analysis

AI is transforming digital forensic science, introducing both opportunities and challenges. The rise of synthetic media – such as deepfakes and AI-generated audio, video, and images – has complicated traditional forensic practices. These technologies undermine core principles like authenticity, traceability, and reproducibility, requiring a shift from static, rule-based methods to dynamic, adaptive frameworks. Conventional approaches, which to date have relied on detecting visual inconsistencies like shadows or compression artefacts, remain useful but are increasingly insufficient against sophisticated manipulations. Modern forensic workflows now integrate AI-powered detection,

DOI: 10.1201/9781003714811-8

multimodal analysis, and real-time processing to keep pace with evolving threats.

As evidenced by current research and practical deployments, outputs from many deepfake detectors and AI-driven forensic tools remain inconsistent, often ambiguous, and require additional supporting evidence to ensure reliability. Developing XAI is therefore crucial (not only for transparency but also for legal admissibility), so that investigators can clearly justify and defend their findings in court.

Addressing synthetic deception also demands cross-disciplinary collaboration, combining expertise in computer vision, linguistics, psychology, and law. Forensic processes must adapt to handle compressed, platform-modified media across diverse formats and languages, while predictive AI models anticipate emerging manipulation techniques before they become widespread.

8.1.1 AI-Driven Efficiency and Advanced Capabilities

AI already delivers substantial benefits to forensic investigations, streamlining processes and enhancing analytical depth. Today, AI automates labour-intensive tasks such as sorting, classifying, and extracting metadata from vast datasets, significantly reducing case timelines and minimising human error. Beyond automation, AI introduces advanced capabilities: machine learning models detect anomalies in logs or network traffic, while LLMs assist with script generation, procedural guidance, and multilingual interpretation of forensic artefacts. In multimedia forensics, AI enables facial recognition, object categorisation, and audio analysis for speaker identification and speech enhancement – critical tools for combating deepfakes and other synthetic threats.

Looking ahead, the focus must expand beyond LLMs towards the broader spectrum of AI and, ultimately, artificial general intelligence (AGI). While LLMs excel at language-based reasoning, future forensic challenges demand systems capable of interpreting multimodal evidence (such as text, images, audio, and behavioural patterns) within complex investigative contexts. AGI offers the promise of adaptive, context-aware intelligence that can autonomously correlate disparate data sources, generate hypotheses, and reason across domains without rigid task constraints [1]. This advancement could enable real-time detection of synthetic media, automated reconstruction of digital timelines, and predictive modelling of emerging cybercrime tactics.

Finding data and interpreting it are fundamentally different tasks: discovery records what exists, while interpretation demands context, accurate time lining, deep artefact knowledge, and the informed judgement of the examiner. When interpretation is delegated to LLMs, practitioners risk mistaking speed for understanding: substituting probabilistic pattern matching for scientific reasoning. Whereas a deliberate, critical integration of AI can instead enable digital forensics to evolve responsibly from reactive analysis towards proactive, evidence-driven intelligence without sacrificing forensic integrity.

8.1.2 Education and Future Readiness

Investigator education on deepfakes and AI must evolve into a dynamic, interdisciplinary, and proactive practice. To strengthen forensic resilience against synthetic media threats, it is essential to consult experts in audio and video forensic analysis and embed their insights into structured training programs. These initiatives should go beyond transferring technical knowledge – they must also integrate industry best practices into DFUs, ensuring investigators remain aligned with evolving evidentiary standards.

AI-driven tools are reshaping this educational landscape by generating interactive teaching materials, quizzes, and simulated scenarios that make forensic training more engaging and adaptive. Solutions such as Semantics 21's "AI Describe" exemplify how automation can reduce psychological strain by handling sensitive content like CSAM while maintaining forensic integrity [2].

Beyond workflow optimisation, these innovations prepare investigators for a rapidly evolving digital environment where deepfakes and complex cyber threats demand adaptive, AI-enhanced methodologies. By combining expert consultation, continuous education, and wellbeing-focused technologies, DFUs can improve future readiness.

Training should address both technical detection and situational interpretation, while promoting tool literacy and hands-on experience. Investigators need direct practice with:

- Deepfake detection suites (open-source and commercial)
- Metadata extraction tools (EXIF, C2PA provenance, hashing)
- Signal-level analysis tools (spectrogram analysis, optical flow, noise profiling)
- AI-assisted triage platforms for social media and live stream investigations

Hands-on environments (i.e. simulated case scenarios) are also essential for building operational proficiency and confidence in real-world applications.

8.2 Rethinking Digital Forensic Methodologies for a Synthetic Future

Detecting synthetic media requires a diverse set of methods, often implemented through multimodal frameworks. Deepfakes, which can seamlessly blend multiple manipulation techniques within a single piece of content, present significant challenges for DFUs. Current detection tools, while increasingly sophisticated, still face limitations, particularly in operational environments where time, resources, and expertise may be constrained.

Multimedia forensics offers a vital response to these challenges by applying scientific techniques to analyse and interpret digital media. It enables investigators to answer key questions about source identification and integrity verification, helping determine the origins/source of specific data and whether it has been altered. Multimedia forensic techniques aim to address several key investigative questions:

- *Source identification*: Determining the origin of the data. Where did it come from? Was it captured by a specific device or distributed through a particular platform?
- *Integrity verification and tampering detection*: Assessing whether the data has been altered. Has it undergone any form of processing, manipulation, or editing that compromises its authenticity?

As synthetic media becomes more prevalent, the forensic process must evolve to include authentication, enhancement, and granular analysis of audio, video, and image content. This is essential not only for investigative accuracy but also for ensuring that digital evidence meets legal standards of reliability and admissibility. Robust forensic and investigative capabilities are essential for distinguishing genuine media from manipulated content and achieving this requires a multi-stakeholder approach.

Collaboration between member states, industry leaders, and academic institutions is critical for advancing detection technologies, sharing expertise, and pooling resources. As Interpol (2024) has stated, only through collective action can we mitigate the harmful impact of synthetic media and preserve the integrity of global law enforcement operations. Deepfake detection exemplifies the need for a layered approach – combining AI-based tools with human expertise to build a reliable evidentiary foundation [3, 4].

While automated systems offer speed and scale, they remain vulnerable to adversarial attacks and evolving generative techniques. Moreover, forensic investigations must go beyond detection; they must produce evidence that withstands judicial scrutiny, requiring reproducibility, explainability, and an unbroken chain of custody. In the absence of universal standards, forensic practice must uphold rigorous principles, recognising that evidence represents an objective truth. Enhancements may clarify visibility (e.g. enhancing video quality), but edits can distort understanding and the media truth – making the role of multimedia forensics indispensable in safeguarding truth in a synthetic future.

The forensic process must uphold rigorous standards, recognising that evidence represents an absolute truth. For example, blood group tests cannot alter biological reality. Similarly, while minor enhancements such as adjusting contrast may clarify a video, editing content fundamentally changes what is visible and, therefore, the truth it conveys.

8.2.1 Formalising Deepfake Investigations: Taxonomy Creation and Standard Operating Procedure (SOP) Integration

As deepfake technologies become increasingly sophisticated and widely accessible, investigators and analysts require structured, repeatable methods to identify and respond to synthetic media. A key approach to achieving this is the development of a deepfake forensic taxonomy: a classification framework that organises manipulated content types, generation techniques, and detection methodologies. A well-defined taxonomy creates a common language across disciplines, enabling law enforcement, researchers, and forensic practitioners to systematically address deepfake-related cases.

If integrated into a forensic workflow, a taxonomy ensures that every stage of the investigation (detection, acquisition, validation, documentation, and evidentiary handling) is supported by appropriate tools, techniques, and classification logic. It can categorise synthetic media by generation method (e.g. GAN-based face swapping, voice cloning, diffusion-based video synthesis), media type (image, video, audio, multimodal), and threat context (e.g. fraud, impersonation, misinformation). When informed by literature reviews and forensic case reports, a taxonomy can provide a foundation for consistent classification and analysis.

For example, the *Deepfake Detection and Analysis Template* shown in Table 8.1 can be adapted to meet specific use-case requirements and towards building a taxonomy.

Table 8.1 Deepfake Detection and Analysis Template

GENERATION METHOD	MEDIA TYPE	THREAT CONTEXT	DETECTION INDICATORS	RECOMMENDED TECHNIQUES
GAN-based Face Swapping	Image, video	Impersonation, organisational fraud, identity manipulation	Facial boundary inconsistencies, texture mismatches, illumination discrepancies, blending artefacts	Frequency-domain analysis, GAN fingerprinting, CNN-based artefact detectors, physiological signal checks (e.g. eye-blink irregularities)
Voice Cloning / Neural Speech Synthesis	Audio	Identity theft, financial fraud, social engineering	Abnormal prosody, spectral irregularities, mismatched emotional tone, unnatural cadence	Advanced audio forensics, spectrogram anomaly detection, voice–identity biometric matching, liveness verification
Diffusion-Based Video Generation / Re-synthesis	Video	Disinformation, propaganda, fabricated evidence	Temporal discontinuities, motion drift, lack of natural micro-expressions, inconsistent motion blur	Frame-level anomaly detection, optical-flow consistency analysis, temporal coherence modelling, diffusion fingerprinting

GENERATION METHOD	MEDIA TYPE	THREAT CONTEXT	DETECTION INDICATORS	RECOMMENDED TECHNIQUES
Multimodal GANs / Transformer-Based Avatars	Image, Audio, Video	Full-avatar impersonation, coordinated disinformation campaigns	Cross-modal inconsistencies (lip–speech mismatch), asynchronous blink/ gesture patterns, mismatched voice–identity cues	Multimodal verification systems, audio–video coherence checks, behavioural biometrics, cross-embedding similarity analysis
Real-Time Deepfake Streaming / Face Re-enactment	Video (live)	Live impersonation, access bypass, phishing	Delayed response timing, unstable facial tracking, frame jitter, unusual head-pose transitions	Real-time liveness detection, edge-based streaming forensics, micro-expression analysis, temporal–spatial anomaly detectors

To demonstrate practical application, an SOP accompanies the taxonomy, outlining a step-by-step process for handling suspected synthetic media. This adaptable template is designed for forensic units, investigative teams, and organisations seeking to formalise their response to deepfake threats.

A step-by-step outline of a hypothetical SOP for forensic workflows is outlined as follows:

Deepfake Forensic SOP: Step-by-Step Workflow

1. *Case Intake and Initial Assessment*
   - *Purpose:* Establish whether the media may be synthetic and assess its potential impact.
   - Steps:
     - o Record case details: source, context, date/time received.
     - o Conduct a preliminary review to identify the media type (image, video, audio, text, or multimodal).
     - o Assess urgency: *Is the content linked to public safety, fraud, reputational harm, or misinformation?*
2. *Media Acquisition and Preservation*
   - *Purpose:* Secure the original media and maintain forensic integrity.
   - Steps:
     - o Acquire the media using validated forensic tools (e.g. FTK Imager, Magnet AXIOM).

- o Generate a cryptographic hash (e.g. SHA-256) to ensure integrity.
- o Extract and preserve metadata (EXIF, file headers, timestamps).
- o Store the media in a secure, access-controlled forensic repository.

3. *Media Classification Using Taxonomy*
   - *Purpose:* Categorise the media to guide analysis and tool selection.
   - Steps:
     - o Classify by media type: image, video, audio, text, or multimodal.
     - o Identify the manipulation technique: face swap, voice synthesis, attribute editing, etc.
     - o Note the suspected generation method: GAN-based, splicing, re-enactment, etc.
4. *Detection and Analysis*
   - *Purpose:* Apply forensic techniques to identify signs of manipulation.
   - Steps:
     - o Use passive techniques: pixel-level analysis, compression artefacts, metadata inconsistencies.
     - o Apply active techniques (if available): watermark verification, provenance tracking (e.g. C2PA standards).
     - o Deploy AI-based tools: CNNs, temporal analysis, physiological signal checks (e.g. FakeCatcher, Deepware Scanner).
     - o Conduct audiovisual consistency checks for multimodal content.
     - o Document all findings with annotated visuals, logs, and tool outputs.
5. *Validation and Cross-Verification*
   - *Purpose:* Confirm findings using multiple methods to ensure reliability.
   - Steps:

- o Repeat analysis using at least two independent forensic tools.
- o Compare results for consistency (e.g. Amped Authenticate vs. Microsoft Video Authenticator).
- o Consult with peer analysts or local DFUs for expert review.

6. *Documentation and Reporting*
   - *Purpose:* Create a comprehensive forensic report suitable for legal or operational use.
   - Steps:
     - o Summarise findings, methods used, and confidence levels.
     - o Include media classification, manipulation indicators, and tool outputs.
     - o Attach hash values, metadata logs, and annotated screenshots.
     - o Ensure the report meets evidential standards for admissibility in court.
7. *Evidentiary Handling and Escalation*
   - *Purpose:* Prepare media and findings for legal, policy, or operational action.
   - Steps:
     - o Maintain a clear chain of custody.
     - o Escalate to legal or communications teams if public statements or takedown requests are needed.
     - o Archive case materials according to retention and compliance policies.
8. *Post-Investigation Review*
   - *Purpose:* Reflect on the investigation and improve future workflows.
   - Steps:
     - o Conduct a debrief with involved teams.
     - o Identify gaps in tools, training, or procedures.
     - o Update SOPs and training materials based on lessons learned.

By following this SOP and integrating a deepfake forensic taxonomy, organisations can move beyond ad hoc responses and establish a repeatable, defensible, and scalable approach to synthetic media investigations. This framework not only supports technical accuracy but also ensures legal and procedural compliance. This is critical in high stakes environments where manipulated content can have serious consequences.

8.3 Future Directions

Understanding the "deepfake dilemma" requires a multi-dimensional approach that goes beyond technical detection. This section explores the four primary themes that frame current discourse on the future direction of deepfake forensics:

8.3.1 Unseen Manipulations: Assessing the True Prevalence of Deepfakes

Despite growing awareness, the actual prevalence of deepfakes in criminal investigations remains uncertain. High-profile cases attract attention, but many instances of media manipulation may go undetected due to limitations in detection capabilities, reporting mechanisms, and practitioner training. This raises critical questions: *Are deepfakes as common as assumed, or are they already influencing investigations without being recognised as synthetic?*

To address this concern, DFUs must receive enhanced training covering both the creation and identification of deepfakes. This should include hands-on experience with current tools and demonstrable use cases across diverse investigative scenarios. Increasing practitioner awareness will enable faster recognition and more accurate assessment of manipulated media. Crucially, DFUs need a comprehensive understanding of the various forms synthetic media can take, supported by clear guidance on assessing authenticity and integrity.

A key priority for future development is the creation of a domain-specific forensic process model, co-designed with law enforcement and forensic professionals. This model should address procedural, technical, and evidentiary challenges associated with synthetic media – including acquisition, validation, analysis, and legal admissibility. Such a framework would help standardise approaches across jurisdictions and ensure forensic practices remain rigorous and defensible in court.

While Chapter 4 explored notable case study examples and Chapter 6 legal and ethical implications, these cases also underscore the uncertainty and confusion faced by legal professionals when encountering synthetic media. Digital literacy plays a significant role in detection capabilities, and its variability can influence outcomes in criminal investigations. There is a pressing need for further research into how deepfakes and other forms of fabricated media impact the criminal justice system, including the diverse ways such content could be introduced as evidence or used to manipulate proceedings.

8.3.2 Mapping Deepfake Incidents and Practitioner Perspectives

As synthetic media becomes increasingly prevalent in criminal investigations, there is a critical need to systematically document the frequency, nature, and context of deepfake occurrences. This includes identifying manipulation techniques, understanding the environments in which they appear, and evaluating the effectiveness of current detection methods. Mapping these patterns is essential for developing forensic tools that are both operationally relevant and technically robust.

As mentioned, a practitioner study, *Deepfake Forensics Survey*[5] explored the operational value and reliability of deepfake detection technologies from the perspective of investigators. Findings revealed significant real-world challenges, including concerns about accuracy, explainability, and lack of validation. While some practitioners expressed cautious optimism about AI-driven detection tools, most remained sceptical of their reliability. These insights underscore the importance of aligning forensic innovation with practitioner experience, ensuring tools are not only technically advanced but also usable and trustworthy in operational settings.

Deepfake technologies challenge traditional forensic methods by introducing highly convincing synthetic content that can evade standard verification techniques. This calls for an update to the forensic literature – one that reflects the evolving nature of multimedia manipulation and integrates deepfake-specific methodologies into broader forensic frameworks. Strengthening this connection will enhance technical understanding and support the development of cohesive tools, training, and policy responses across sectors.

Finally, the relationship between deepfake analysis and multimedia forensics requires clearer articulation within academic and professional discourse. Although both fields share a focus on the authentication and integrity of digital media, they are often treated as distinct domains. This fragmentation can hinder detection and response efforts. A more integrated approach – bridging deepfake forensics with multimedia forensic principles – will help build a unified foundation for tackling synthetic media threats in a rapidly digitising world.

Building on these findings [5], a more comprehensive dataset that includes input from more police forces and DFUs, along with detailed case examples of deepfake incidents, would enable the creation of reference use-cases and generate more robust, citable statistics.

8.3.3 Advancing Detection and Shaping Perceptions

Given the fact that deepfake technologies continue to evolve, the need for efficient, scalable, and reliable detection techniques has never been greater. However, technical innovation alone is insufficient. A key challenge lies in ensuring that these tools are usable, trustworthy, and impactful across multiple sectors, including education, law enforcement, digital forensics, and policymaking. Designing solutions that are both operationally relevant and ethically sound requires understanding how different stakeholders interact with detection systems and what constraints they face in real-world environments.

Equally important is the need to reshape public and professional perceptions of deepfakes and fabricated media. Awareness must extend beyond facial synthesis or voice cloning to encompass the full spectrum of manipulation techniques. Education initiatives should promote critical media consumption, equip individuals to question authenticity, and demonstrate real-world use cases to foster trust in forensic processes. Global efforts reflect this growing priority: curriculum reforms in the UK will introduce AI and misinformation awareness from 2028, while Finland, Singapore, and the Netherlands have launched national media literacy campaigns. UNESCO and the European Commission have also issued guidance on integrating AI and misinformation awareness into education policy. These initiatives underscore a clear consensus: public engagement is foundational to societal resilience in the age of synthetic media [6].

8.3.4 Public Engagement and Responsibility of Organisations

Research shows that the human ability to detect deepfakes is far less reliable than previously assumed, exposing a critical vulnerability in collective media literacy [7]. As synthetic media becomes more convincing and accessible, public awareness and education emerge as essential components of a broader strategy to combat misinformation. An informed public can serve as an important line of defence – scrutinising digital content, questioning authenticity, and reporting suspected manipulations.

Organisations also play a pivotal role in fostering media literacy by embedding deepfake awareness into cybersecurity and IT training frameworks. As deepfakes increasingly enable impersonation and social engineering attacks, these educational efforts must be proactive, practical, and widely accessible. Building resilience against deepfake-enabled threats requires a combination of technical safeguards and human vigilance. Recommended measures include:

- *Adopt a zero-trust approach to digital media:* Treat all audio, video, and image content as potentially manipulated. Implement robust verification protocols for sensitive communications, financial transactions, and high stakes decision-making to prevent exploitation.
- *Comprehensive employee training and awareness campaigns*: Equip staff to identify deepfake-related threats such as voice phishing (vishing), synthetic identity fraud, and CEO impersonation scams. Use simulated attack scenarios to build readiness and establish clear protocols for validating identities during business interactions, both online and offline.
- *Critical evaluation of online sources and narratives:* Encourage employees to question the authenticity of digital content and rely on trusted verification services such as BBC Verify or Intel Fact Checker.
- *Technical safeguards:*
  - o Watermarking: Embed digital watermarks in official media to signal authenticity.
  - o Blockchain for Corporate Media*:* Use blockchain-based solutions to ensure provenance and integrity of organisational content.

By combining policy, technology, and education, organisations can significantly reduce the risk of deepfake-enabled attacks and strengthen overall cyber resilience.

8.4 Open Research Questions and Emerging Themes

In addition to the previous points, several research questions remain with regards to advancing deepfake forensics:

- Can a unified methodology for deepfake forensic analysis be established?
- How can reproducibility be ensured, so that identical actions consistently yield the same results?
- How can we make deepfake detection models explainable for legal and forensic contexts? What role can XAI play in advancing forensic reliability?
- How can detection models maintain high accuracy across different platforms, compression levels, and resolutions without retraining for each scenario?
- How can we effectively detect deepfakes that combine multiple modalities (e.g. audio-video synchronisation, lip-sync manipulation)?

Addressing these questions is essential to further advance deepfake forensic science and methods in the future. As such, we will investigate these issues further in the following section.

8.4.1 Standardisation and Explainability in Forensics

To establish a unified methodology for deepfake forensic analysis and ensure reproducibility (where identical actions consistently yield the same results), standardised benchmarks and peer-reviewed protocols are essential. Research must evolve alongside forensic practice, incorporating domain-specific methodologies, structured training frameworks, and policy guidance tailored to synthetic media threats. By integrating technical innovation with stakeholder engagement and public education, the field can progress towards a more resilient and informed approach to deepfake forensics.

Current detection tools face notable limitations, including inconsistent outputs, ambiguous interpretations, and reliance on narrow training datasets. In forensic contexts, explainability is critical for reliability and legal admissibility. Embedding XAI into forensic workflows can address these challenges by producing transparent, interpretable results that strengthen trust and evidential integrity.

XAI offers promising avenues for enhancing transparency in detection processes. Much like "showing your working" in mathematics, XAI enables forensic analysts to interpret and justify AI-generated outputs, thereby strengthening trust, accountability, and evidential reliability in legal contexts. Tools such as Magnet Verify exemplify this approach, conducting structural analyses of media files to assess origin, detect manipulation, and present findings in a defensible format. Despite these advances, gaps remain – fabricated media is increasingly exploited across sectors, from false identity documents to fraudulent reporting mechanisms, yet few preventive measures exist without active intervention.

In order to improve upon standardisation and XAI, we need to:

- Create interpretable detectors that show *why* content is classified as fake, supporting expert review and legal admissibility.
- Evaluate how humans interact with automated detectors, including confidence calibration and decision-support systems.

8.1.2 Dataset Diversity and Hybrid Forensic Models

Addressing linguistic diversity is a critical challenge in deepfake detection, particularly for audio and multimodal approaches. Representative datasets must account for the nuances of different languages, especially in techniques relying on lip sync or speech artefacts [8]. Moreover, deepfakes often involve multiple types of fabrication, necessitating multimodal datasets and hybrid forensic paradigms that integrate classical signal processing with machine learning classifiers trained to detect statistical irregularities, frequency-domain anomalies, and neural fingerprints specific to generative AI architectures.

Continuous model retraining and dataset curation are essential to maintain detection efficacy as generative technologies evolve. By training classifiers on large corpora of synthetic and authentic content, forensic analysts can develop models capable of identifying spatial inconsistencies, latent vector artefacts, and other manipulation signatures. Ensuring model generalisation and resilience against adversarial adaptation will be key to future-proofing forensic capabilities. As such, we will need to:

- Develop detectors resilient to compression artefacts, low-resolution uploads, streaming formats, and post-processing filters.
- Explore domain-generalisable models capable of performing reliably across platforms such as TikTok, YouTube, and messaging apps.

8.4.3 Expanding Preventive Strategies and Collaborative Initiatives

Beyond detection, the field must prioritise proactive prevention and collaborative innovation to stay ahead of emerging threats. Initiatives such as deepfake competitions and workshops (exemplified by the UK Deepfake Challenge, global Deepfake workshops, e.g. LJMU Deepfake Forensics workshop (2023) and Deepfake Forensics 2.0 workshop in (2026 [9]) and ACM (Association for Computer Machinery) Deepfake Forensics Workshop (2025 and 2026), are essential for accelerating research, benchmarking detection tools, and fostering cross-sector collaboration between academia, industry, and law enforcement. These events provide a safe environment for experimentation, encourage creative problem-solving, and help establish standardised evaluation metrics, ensuring consistency and comparability across solutions.

In parallel, emerging defensive strategies represent a paradigm shift from reactive detection to proactive resilience. Techniques such as adversarial watermarking, invisible secure watermark perturbations (ISWP), and data poisoning such as Nightshade embed security directly into media assets and training datasets. By integrating these approaches, the community can reduce the risk of synthetic content proliferation and manipulation at its source. This shift towards prevention, combined with collaborative benchmarking efforts, will be critical for building robust, trustworthy systems capable of mitigating the evolving challenges posed by deepfake technologies. Therefore, to improve preventative strategies and future collaboration, the following are recommended:

- Investigate "fingerprinting" of generative architectures and watermarking-based provenance tracking.

- Introduce standardised, community-driven benchmarks to compare and evaluate forensics methods consistently.

8.4.4 Deepfake Detection and Prevention: Key Challenges and Solutions

At its core, this work reveals that deepfake forensics faces complex challenges across technical, legal, and societal domains (Table 8.2). While detection technologies are advancing, gaps in standardisation, governance, and public awareness persist. Addressing these issues requires a multi-layered approach combining technical innovation, regulatory frameworks, and education. Deepfake forensics is evolving around five main pillars:

1. *Detection*: Identifying manipulated media using specialist deepfake detectors and AI-driven techniques.
2. *Attribution and recognition*: Linking deepfakes to their source models or creators.
3. *Passive authentication*: Detecting inconsistencies without embedding prior security measures.
4. *Active authentication*: Using watermarks or cryptographic signatures to verify authenticity.
5. R*ealistic scenarios*: Handling compressed, noisy, or low quality media typical of social platforms, detecting within realistic use cases and scenarios.

It is essential to consider the wide range of use cases and data formats in which deepfakes can appear, adopting a collaborative approach to effectively address these challenges. An innovative example tackling both audio and video aspects of deepfake media is the *MSc in Audio and Video Forensics*, developed by LJMU School of Engineering in consultation with Merseyside Police. Led by Dr Karl Jones (Applied Forensic Technology Research Group), this programme brings together leading experts in audio and video analysis, ensuring students gain advanced technical skills alongside practical forensic methodologies. Through undertaking the MSc, Merseyside Police now have one of the most highly trained audio/video forensic units in the UK.

Table 8.2 Challenges and Potential Solutions

DOMAIN	MAIN CHALLENGES	POTENTIAL SOLUTIONS
Technical	• Inconsistent detection outputs and lack of reproducibility • Limited dataset diversity (languages, modalities) • Vulnerability to adversarial adaptation • Limited training models for academic works • Lack of explainability for legal admissibility • Preventive strategies not widely adopted	• Develop standardised forensic protocols and benchmarks • Expand multilingual and multimodal datasets • Continuous model retraining and hybrid forensic models • Promote release of training models for comparison and evaluation • Embed XAI in workflows • Implement adversarial watermarking and AI poisoning techniques
Legal	• Absence of unified global standards for forensic evidence • Privacy concerns over watermarking and perturbations • Cross-border enforcement gaps • Unclear liability for platforms and perpetrators	• Harmonise laws and evidentiary standards internationally • Create privacy-compliant watermarking frameworks • Define platform accountability under digital service regulations
Societal and Policy	• Low media literacy and susceptibility to misinformation • Lack of structured training for legal professionals and law enforcement • Cultural and linguistic inclusivity gaps • Limited industry collaboration on provenance tracking	• Launch public awareness campaigns and media literacy programs • Develop training frameworks for judiciary and law enforcement • Promote inclusive datasets and detection tools • Incentivise industry adoption of watermarking and blockchain provenance systems

The complexity of these challenges shows that no single solution can fully address the risks posed by deepfakes. Instead, progress depends on an integrated ecosystem where technical innovation aligns with legal governance and societal preparedness. Standardisation efforts must be coupled with XAI to ensure forensic outputs are transparent and admissible in court. At the same time, preventive strategies (such as watermarking and provenance tracking) should be embedded into media creation pipelines to reduce manipulation at its source. Collaborative initiatives between academia, industry, and law enforcement will be essential for benchmarking tools and sharing best practices, while public education and professional training can strengthen resilience against misinformation.

A key priority moving forward is the development of real-time deepfake detection systems capable of operating across social media and live-streaming environments, where manipulated content spreads quickly and can shape public perception within minutes. These systems must be scalable, interoperable with platform APIs, and capable of triage at platform speed, enabling suspicious material to be flagged or isolated before it achieves widespread reach. Equally important is the rise of deepfake threats within professional and organisational contexts, where they are facilitating fraud, impersonation, and targeted disinformation. Reliable, real-time verification tools for video conferencing, digital identity authentication, and internal communication channels will therefore be essential to preserving organisational security and trust.

Taken together, these directions underscore the need to reconceptualise deepfake detection as a continuous, adaptive process rather than a fixed technical solution: one that integrates robust machine-learning practices with real-world deployment constraints, adversarial threat models, and evidentiary requirements.

8.5 Summary

The rise of deepfake technologies is fundamentally reshaping the landscape of digital forensics, demanding a re-evaluation of traditional methodologies to remain effective. Emerging directions (such as mapping deepfake incidents, integrating practitioner insights, and uncovering the hidden prevalence of manipulated content) underscore the urgency of interdisciplinary collaboration and technological innovation. Addressing dataset diversity, ensuring reproducibility, and embedding transparency into forensic workflows will be critical for legal admissibility and public trust. Ultimately, digital forensic science must not only respond to evolving threats but also anticipate them, ensuring that the pursuit of truth remains resilient in an era defined by digital deception.

References

[1] N. Niță and C. Apreutesei, 'Artificial Intelligence, challenges and transformative opportunities of Forensic Science', *Acta Universitatis George Bacovia: Juridica*, vol. 14, no. 1, pp. 57–69, Jan. 2025. Available: http://juridica.ugb.ro/-NeluNIȚĂ,CătălinAPREUTESEI

[2] Semantics 21, 'The world's most advanced AI platform for CSAM categorisation and victim identification', *Semantics 21*. Available: www.semantics21.com/s21-visionx/.
[3] Interpol, 'Beyond illusions: Unmasking the threat of synthetic media for law enforcement', Lyon, France, Jun. 2024. Available: www.interpol.int/en/News-and-Events/News/2024/Beyond-illusions-Unmasking-the-threat-of-synthetic-media-for-law-enforcement
[4] Á. MacDermott, 'Ctrl+Alt+deceit: Policing the deepfake dilemma', Forensic Science International: Digital Investigation, DFRWS EU 2026-Selected Papers from the 13th Annual Digital Forensics Research Conference Europe, 56, March. 2026.
[5] Á. MacDermott, 'Deepfake forensic survey dataset', Liverpool John Moores University. Dataset available via JISC. LJMU Ethics Approval Reference: 25/CMP/004, October 2025.
[6] UNESCO, 'Artificial intelligence in education', Available: www.unesco.org/en/digital-education/artificial-intelligence.
[7] N. C. Köbis, B. Doležalová, and I. Soraperra, 'Fooled twice: People cannot detect deepfakes but think they can', *iScience*, vol. 24, no. 11, Nov. 2021, doi: 10.1016/j.isci.2021.103364.
[8] G. Bendiab, H. Haiouni, I. Moulas, and S. Shiaeles, 'Deepfakes in digital media forensics: Generation, AI-based detection and challenges', *Journal of Information Security and Applications*, vol. 88, Feb. 2025, doi: 10.1016/j.jisa.2024.103935.
[9] Á. MacDermott, 'Deepfake forensics: Exploring the impact and implications of fabricated media in digital forensic investigations – DFRWS EU poster', in *Digital Forensics Research Workshop Europe (DFRWS EU 2025). Brno, Czech Republic*, 2025. Accessed: Apr. 03, 2025. Available: https://dfrws.org/wp-content/uploads/2025/04/DFRWS_EU_2025_paperposter_115.pdf.

Index

D

E

Q

For Product Safety Concerns and Information please contact our EU representative GPSR@taylorandfrancis.com
Taylor & Francis Verlag GmbH, Kaufingerstraße 24, 80331 München, Germany

www.ingramcontent.com/pod-product-compliance
Lightning Source LLC
LaVergne TN
LVHW011155030926
847199LV00028B/299
9781041200505